RECENT INITIATIVES IN COMMUNICATION IN THE HUMANITIES

British Library Cataloguing in Publication Data

Katzen, May
  Recent initiatives in communication in the
  humanities.——(Library and information research
  reports, ISSN 0263-1709; 11)
  1. Communication in the humanities——Great
  Britain   2. Humanities——Information services
  ——Great Britain   3. Humanities——
  Information services——United States
  I. Title   II. Howley, S.M.   III. British
  Library.*Research and Development Department*
  IV. Series
  025'.060013'072041   AZ188.G7

  ISBN 0-7123-3016-X

RECENT INITIATIVES IN COMMUNICATION IN THE HUMANITIES

M Katzen and SM Howley

Library and Information Research Report 11

Abstract

This report comprises a number of contributions concerned with recent activities in humanities communication in the UK and the USA. It includes an account of an Anglo-American conference held on the topic in May 1982. It also covers some initiatives which took place subsequently — in particular, a visit to the USA by Dr Katzen, the establishment in the UK of the Office for Humanities Communication and a proposal to the American Council of Learned Societies for the establishment of an Office of Scholarly Communication and Technology in the USA. In addition, it contains a select bibliography.

Library and Information Research Reports are published by the British Library and distributed by Publications Section, British Library Lending Division, Boston Spa, Wetherby, West Yorkshire, LS23 7BQ.

ISBN 0 7123 3016 X
ISSN 0263-1709

The opinions expressed in this report are those of the authors and not necessarily those of the British Library.

Typeset by Type Out, London, SW16 2AS and printed in Great Britain at the University Press, Cambridge.

iv

Keywords

Humanities communication
Scholarly activity
Communication research
Anglo-American cooperation

Contents

List of figures

Authors

Dr M Katzen   Project Manager
Office for Humanities Communication
University of Leicester

Mrs SM Howley Project Officer
British Library Research and Development
Department

Acknowledgements

The authors would like to express their gratitude to colleagues on both sides of the Atlantic for their help and advice. Special thanks are due to the American Council of Learned Societies for sponsoring the Cawthorpe House meeting and for allowing publication of the paper by Dr Herbert C Morton, which appears as Chapter 5.

The authors would also like to thank Mrs Margaret Mann for editing the report and compiling the bibliography.

Foreword

Research in the humanities is an international enterprise. This is especially so in the case of research workers in the USA and the UK, who share a common language and common cultural traditions. It is evident that many of the problems which affect the humanities communication system in both countries are sufficiently similar to warrant joint discussion and joint action. It is gratifying therefore to be associated with this report which describes recent developments in each country, details the first major attempt to discuss these problems together, and points the way to further collaboration in the future.

Thomas A Noble
Executive Associate
American Council of Learned Societies

1 Introduction

This report deals with a number of recent developments related to the communication of research in the humanities. It touches on matters affecting research in the humanities as scholarly disciplines, but mainly discusses communication research focused on the humanities (rather than on science and technology or the social sciences). The contents will be of interest to three main groups: humanities scholars, information scientists and members of funding agencies concerned with these matters. Since information scientists have mostly been trained in science and technology, they are often puzzled by the difference between the aims, methods and orientation of research workers in the humanities as distinct from other disciplines. Likewise, most humanities researchers are ignorant of the vocabulary, content and scope of information science and communication research. To avoid confusion and misunderstanding, it is worth devoting a little time to an attempt at definitions.

What is meant by 'the humanities'? The term dates back to the Renaissance, and the Humanists, whence its core meaning of the study of the classics (as opposed to theology) and, by extension, the study of essentially human, rather than divine, matters. This is the meaning attributed to the term by the 1955 edition of *The shorter Oxford English dictionary:* 'Learning or literature concerned with human culture, as grammar, rhetoric, poetry and especially the ancient Latin and Greek classics'; a definition reproduced (excluding the examples) in the new (1982) edition of the *Concise Oxford dictionary*.

Another recent Oxford dictionary (*St Michael Oxford dictionary*, 1981) provides other useful associations in its definition: 'Arts subjects (especially study of the Greek and Latin classics) as opposed to the sciences', indicating that the term is one essentially related to the divisions between academic disciplines, and that it refers not only to certain kinds of subject matter, but, equally importantly, to a particular set of methods, distinct from those used in scientific disciplines.

As these examples suggest, 'the humanities' is a term whose boundaries have shifted with time, and one which is to be understood in an inclusive, rather than an exclusive sense. It is perhaps more widely used and more easily understood in the USA and in Europe than in the UK. This is partly due to the fact that in the USA there have been two major Commissions on the Humanities (which reported in 1964 and 1980, respectively). The result of the first Commission was the setting up of a separate federal funding agency devoted to the financial support of this branch of learning, the National Endowment for the Humanities (NEH). A recent (1982) definition provided by the American Council on Education in a survey of the financial support for the humanities, sponsored by the NEH, indicates the subject range of the term as it is interpreted at present by the NEH:

> 'Humanities' includes the following fields of study: language, both modern and classical; linguistics; literature; history (including history of science); jurisprudence (the theory, history and philosophy of law, rather than professional legal study); philosophy (including philosophy of science); archaeology; comparative religion; ethics; the history, criticism and theory of the arts (excluding performing arts); and those disciplines and interdisciplinary programs which are humanistic in content or method (such as anthropology, American studies and ethnic and women's studies).

Useful though such a comprehensive list is, it also raises new questions: in particular, how the boundary lines between the humanities and the social sciences might usefully be drawn. For a satisfactory elucidation of what (for want of a better word) one can only call the 'flavour' of the humanities, the ideals and aspirations of those who pursue this scholarly calling, one can do no better than to turn to the opening chapter of the report of the last Commission on the Humanities [1], which sets out the scope and orientation of this branch of knowledge:

> Through the humanities, we reflect on the fundamental question: what does it mean to be human .... They reveal how people have tried to make moral, spiritual and intellectual sense of a world in which irrationality, despair, loneliness and death are as conspicuous as birth, friendship, hope and reason. We learn how individuals or societies define the moral life and try to attain it, attempt to reconcile freedom and the responsibilities of citizenship and express themselves artistically ... awakening a sense of what it might be like to be someone else or to live in another time or culture ....

> The humanities presume particular methods of expression and inquiry — language, dialogue, reflection, imagination and metaphor .... The aims of these activities of mind are not geometric proof and quantitative measure, but rather insight, perspective, critical understanding, discrimination and creativity .... The humanities remain dedicated to the disciplined development of verbal, perceptual and imaginative skills needed to understand experience.

In defining the fields of knowledge encompassed by the humanities, the Commission regarded languages and literature, history and philosophy as 'the central humanistic fields' and accepted also the additional fields covered by the NEH. But it stressed that 'fields alone do not define the humanities', quoting from a speech by Charles Frankel in 1978 that 'the humanities are that form of knowledge in which the knower is revealed. All knowledge becomes humanistic ... when we are asked to contemplate not only the proposition but the proposer'.

The Commission continued:

Whether defined by questions, methods or fields, the humanities employ a particular medium and turn of mind. The medium is language. Discourse sets in motion and supports reflection and judgement. The humanities have close ties not only with speech but especially with writing and the thought processes writing makes possible .... Study cannot proceed without creating and using texts .... The turn of mind is towards history ....

The essence of the humanities is a spirit or an attitude toward humanity. They show how the individual is autonomous and at the same time bound in the ligatures of language and history to humankind across time and throughout the world.

We make no apology for quoting so extensively from the report of the Humanities Commission because we believe that its statements not only define, but are a noble expression of, what the humanities can and should be.

The main subject of this report is not the content of scholarship in the humanities, but those social processes which enable scholarship to take place and to be communicated to others. As in all fields of knowledge, these communication processes are concerned with information transfer — the creation, storage, retrieval and dissemination of information. These processes intermesh, and constitute a system of interconnected, but functionally distinct, parts. This communication system enables both the raw materials and the products of scholarly activity to be transferred across time and place. The system, therefore, constitutes the social context and the essential framework for scholarship. Communication is facilitated by a number of institutions, two important examples of which are libraries and other information services, and publishers.

This volume is concerned with recent developments which have taken place on both sides of the Atlantic and which were intended to improve the system of communication in the humanities in both the USA and the UK. These developments include discussions of the causes of malfunction in the system as well as positive steps which are being taken to bring about improvements. Inevitably, there is some repetition of information where the various reports cover the same ground, but it was thought best to leave them as far as possible in their original form.

1.1 Reference

1 *The humanities in American life. Report of the Commission on the Humanities.* Berkeley, Los Angeles, London, University of California Press, 1980.

2 Communication in the humanities: report by S M Howley on an Anglo-American Conference held at Cawthorpe House, Lincolnshire, May 1982

2.1 Preliminaries

One sunny weekend in May 1982, 17 people (eight based in the USA and nine in the UK) descended on a fine Georgian house for a conference on communication in the humanities. The location was Cawthorpe House, Bourne, near Peterborough, England. The conference was organised by Professor AJ Meadows of the University of Leicester and funded by the American Council of Learned Societies (ACLS).

Why communication in the humanities and why a joint UK/USA seminar?

For some time, various parties on both sides of the Atlantic had been aware that, despite recent efforts, humanities remained the poor relation both of the sciences and the social sciences with regard to understanding of, investigation into and funding relating to problems in the communication of research. At the same time, change and innovation were affecting a whole range of communication activities in the humanities — academic library budgets were being restricted; publishers of scholarly monographs were cutting back on production; and new technology was providing a vast and under-explored range of challenges and opportunities. It seemed to the organisers and funders, therefore, that there was an urgent need for a conference at which could be discussed the various problems currently facing the communication of humanities research, especially those related to financial or technological pressures.

From the outset, a joint Anglo-American discussion had been envisaged, on the assumption that enough similarity existed between the two countries to permit meaningful discussion, whilst differences were sufficient to stimulate thought. In addition, interaction between the two countries in humanities research is considerable — the number of American scholars whose research requires a trip to the UK, for example, is probably not much greater than the number of British scholars making the reverse pilgrimage. This suggests that the questions raised by communication in the humanities could fruitfully be examined cooperatively and also that any resulting projects and activities might equally fruitfully be conducted cooperatively.

The last point is an important one, because the aim of the conference was to be more than a 'talking-shop', to do more than increase our understanding of the present and possible future state of research on humanities communication (although this would be a considerable achievement in itself). The aim was to influence that future by producing recommendations which would be acted upon. Hence the participants were selected not just because they represented specialisms such as research funding and administration, academic research, libraries, learned societies and publishing, but also because of their ability, through influence or direct initiation, to shape the future of the communication system in the humanities.

A list of participants is given in Section 2.8 of this report.

The conference ran from the evening of Friday, 7 May to the lunchtime of the following Monday, 10 May 1982. The programme is given as Section 2.9, but, it should be added, more to give the reader the same pre-knowledge of the event as had the participants than to indicate what actually happened! Brief introductions to the main items on the agenda were indeed duly given by those indicated on the programme, but most of the meeting was devoted to discussion which, despite the efforts of gifted chairmen, ranged far and wide, usually failing to address itself to the questions (reproduced in Section 2.9) which acted as guidelines to the sessions, succeeding brilliantly in answering a good many others, but, never, ever, for one single moment, being dull.

The following sections attempt to give the reader some flavour of the proceedings at each session rather than to produce verbatim accounts. It is a pity that it is outside the remit of this report to recount the contribution to Anglo-American understanding made outside the scheduled sessions. Suffice it to say that the facilities provided by Cawthorpe House and its beautiful grounds provided the perfect restorative counterpoint to the rigours of what were, indeed, some very demanding discussions.

2.2 Retrospective review of research into humanities communication

The first substantive session, on the Saturday morning, aimed to establish an agreed foundation from which the discussion could grow and addressed itself to the following questions:

(a) what has been learnt from previous studies?
(b) what have been the problems of implementing research findings?
(c) to what extent have financial considerations hindered both the research and its implementation?
(d) have there been difficulties in finding qualified research personnel and interested institutions?

In the event, the answers to these questions were found to interact closely. Research into the information and communication aspects of the humanities and social sciences seemed to teach us that there was a lack of interest in information on the part of academics. This lack of interest was one important reason why research findings had not been widely implemented. It was crucial to locate and encourage suitable individuals both to carry out the research, on the one hand, and to disseminate it and implement it, on the other. A vicious circle tended to exist — in the USA, for example, the humanities were at a severe disadvantage in Washington because there was no capacity to collect and analyse data centrally, whilst, because of lack of political muscle, there was insufficient power to implement recommendations (i.e. those in the National Enquiry) that such data should be collected.

Good people and good ideas — these were crucial, but it would be wrong to dismiss totally the importance of financial constraint.

In both the UK and the USA, the governments were not particularly sympathetic either to the humanities or to new national activities, but shortage of funds for new public endeavours could well be a long-term trend not related to the political complexion of individuals in power.

But where and how were 'suitable individuals' to be found? From the library and information science community? From the humanities? Or from elsewhere? In the USA, the Council on Library Resources (CLR) has introduced new schemes in an attempt to improve the quality of people in library and information science and interest them in wider issues. But are these the most appropriate people to carry out research into communication in the humanities? Humanities scholars are more likely to be interested in research into their own subject areas than in research into humanities communication. The feeling of the conference was that the latter type of research probably did not have much esteem within humanities circles. On the other hand, there *was* a strong tradition which bestowed esteem upon the compilation of a bibliography — indeed, the scholar and the bibliographer were often the same person.

On the whole, however, there was lack of interest in research into humanities communication. Was this likely to change without any special effort from bodies such as those represented at the conference? Two factors were potentially very important in this respect — the worsening economic situation and the growing importance of 'new technology'. Some members of the conference felt that the worsening economic situation would lead to decreased opportunities for humanities research *per se* and the existence of opportunities for research into humanities communication might well, in such a situation, attract the humanities researcher. New technology was, inevitably, going to be an important element of future research into humanities communication, both as a topic for research and as a technique to assist research. This might deter humanities researchers in the short-term, but attract them in the long-term as a new generation of more technology-oriented researchers emerged.

After some discussion, the conference decided that research into humanities communication was best carried out by a mix of people with backgrounds in the humanities and in librarianship and information science. The ideal situation would be one where the research team was led by a senior scholar in the humanities.

How could interest be stimulated amongst such people so that they might be enthused to carry out such research or at least to be receptive to its results? Various methods were discussed. 'Demonstration projects' which involved humanities scholars being exposed to new systems of retrieving information were mentioned, but things were not helped here, some thought, by the lack of user-friendly systems in the humanities. The British Library Research and Development (BLR&D) Department had in the past organised seminars in the hope of stimulating interest in information and communication on the part of humanities academics. The Department's experience led it to conclude that seminars on specific areas (such as that on art history) were more successful than general ones.

The discussion on how and to what extent people from outside both the humanities *and* librarianship and information science might be involved had an added dimension to it since many of those at the conference had subject backgrounds outside these areas — there were physicists, chemists and biologists present, for example.

This was probably quite significant — scientists are more information-aware than humanities scholars. Twenty years ago, however, they were as indifferent as the humanities people are now. If humanities communication is at the same stage as scientific communication was in the 1960s, it ought to be possible to plan the development of humanities communication in such a way that the pitfalls which beset the development of scientific communication can be avoided.

Sir Harry Hookway, who chaired this opening session, concluded it by pointing out the importance of the three 'i's — influence, interest and infectivity. Developments could not be significantly influenced unless senior and respected scholars in the humanities could be converted — the pioneers must be acceptable. Interest would then be generated amongst other humanities scholars. For progress to be rapid, however, the focus must be on activities that are likely to spread — hence the importance of 'infectivity'.

2.3 The problems of research workers in the humanities as originators and users of information

Obviously, there is a whole range of problems facing the academic researcher in the humanities (for example, political freedom in both the UK and the USA is supposedly a reality, but uncertainty over tenure can create its own form of unacceptable control). The conference concentrated, however, on matters directly connected with the origination and use of information.

2.3.1 Knowledge of materials

Here it was necessary to distinguish between primary and secondary material. Some present thought that primary material did not pose a problem, although others felt that knowledge of the existence and availability of resources plus difficulties in obtaining travel funds were problems. On the matter of access to secondary material, a spectrum was identified with, at the one end of it, those who felt they had to read everything, and, at the other, those who appeared to rely exclusively on reading primary materials and on the 'invisible college'.

2.3.2 Getting published

Despite the decreasing number of titles being published, getting published was still not seen as being a problem for the older and established scholar. It was a problem, however, for the younger scholar. Publishers were often not interested in the topics on which the younger scholar wanted to write. An academic at the conference expressed the belief that publishers were mainly responsible for deciding on which topics books would be published — scholars, flattered at being asked to write a book, usually went along with the chosen topic.

2.3.3 New technology

The conference discussed this matter for some time, but it was not always clear whether they thought it solved or created problems and the attitudes expressed varied from extreme optimism to extreme pessimism. Some concern was expressed that new technology, in its applications both for information retrieval and for document generation and reproduction, posed problems of 'quality control'. The expression 'garbage in, garbage out' was used more than once and a distinction drawn between 'busy' and 'clever' — new technology might (or might not) make the researcher less busy, but it certainly did not necessarily make him more clever.

On the matter of information retrieval, some were of the opinion that the need for speed and the dangers of duplication were not as great for the humanities as for other areas. Not as much money was involved and individuals tended to work as individuals, not as teams. All these factors, some thought, meant that improved methods of information retrieval would not necessarily have much impact on the methods of research used by humanities researchers. (However, access to bibliographies *was* regarded as important and reviews were felt to be a potentially very useful resource, not at present fully exploited.) Also on the more cautious side of the debate, views were expressed (from both sides of the Atlantic) that many humanities researchers had a horror of being swamped by irrelevant information and a horror that the computer might well increase the danger.

The above can be typified as the position of healthy cynicism taken by some present. Others were not so certain that, for example, workers in the humanities did not value speed. It was pointed out, for example, that there were many complaints when the publication schedule of the Modern Language Association (MLA) bibliography fell behind and also that humanists had deadlines — conferences to be prepared for, publication deadlines to be met — just as much as anyone else.

There was much discussion and exchange of information on the use of word processors and other relatively new methods for the creation of documents and much speculation about possible future developments.

Were researchers in the humanities likely to embrace the new technology? It was pointed out, as a factor operating against the likelihood of this, that university staff in the humanities were aging and their immobility increasing. In such a situation, there was a danger of stagnation and loss of confidence, of retrenchment rather than the adoption of new methods.

The conference then identified two means by which resistance to new technology by humanists might be reduced — one being action by the learned societies and the other courses (perhaps summer schools) at which young scholars in the humanities would be introduced to the applications of new technology.

2.4 The dissemination of humanities research to a wider audience

This session took place after dinner on the Saturday evening and was characterised by a certain levity that no doubt owed something to a reaction to the long and hard discussions that had gone on throughout the day and a great deal to the splendid dinner laid on by Cawthorpe House.

The American contingent was, on the whole, fairly optimistic that, in the USA, the humanities were beginning to win the battle for acceptance. Schoolchildren now recognised the word 'humanist' as applying to a practitioner in the humanities and there was a growing awareness in the public mind — the huge audiences for the Jefferson lectures were taken as evidence of this. Much, however, remained to be done. The fourth chapter of *The humanities in American life* had concentrated on the humanities and community and private life — museums, public libraries, television, radio, etc. — and had generated a formidable list of prescriptions. The problem was not one of shortage of ideas but, again, of implementation. There was a large measure of approval for the contention that, to a large extent, an obligation rested on the humanists themselves and that financial and intellectual support would come more readily if people could be convinced that the humanities were not a spectator sport.

It was also felt that, on both sides of the Atlantic, exposure in the media, especially on television, was a crucial matter. The suggestion was made that different branches of the humanities are not equally presented on television — archaeology, for example, has relatively more exposure than the others — and that scholars should strive for more exposure for their particular subjects since it would stimulate the interest of potential students and potential funders.

Who should present the humanities on television? Professional communicators or scholars? Some present favoured the first alternative, but others pointed out that educators can also be entertaining, that some researchers are good communicators and that the idea of a headmaster teaching through the mass media is in no way intrinsically unacceptable.

Inevitably, at this point, discussion directed itself to the dividing line between the research area in the humanities and the general media/entertainment area. It was agreed that this dividing line was blurred and difficult to draw. It had long ago been pointed out, for example, that Robert Graves was basically writing up his research when he wrote *The white goddess.*

Another relevant question was that of exactly what research gets through to schools and universities and into textbooks. How long does it take research to be communicated in this way? Upper-level textbooks are often written by original researchers and lower-level ones by school-teachers — is this the right way round?

Exactly how does the communication network in the humanities operate? Should learned societies be doing more, on behalf of their members, to exploit the opportunities offered by the media? How do teachers link in with learned societies? From where do school-teachers get their opinions? The content of book reviews and the criteria for selection of books for review were obviously crucial, since they could affect people's perceptions of what was happening in a subject.

The session continued to raise a host of fascinating questions such as these and it was a pity that, by that late hour, there was neither the time nor the energy to pursue them! However, all were certain that the answers to some of these questions were simply not known and further investigation of them was required, but this brought the conference back to the question raised in the first session of finding the appropriate people to carry out the investigations.

It was also agreed that the time was particularly ripe to consider the question of dissemination of humanities research to a wider audience and, in particular, the general public. This was partly because the humanities often relate closely to people's leisure-time pursuits and people, through choice or otherwise, have increasing amounts of leisure time available. But it was also because the diversity of routes by which the humanities can impact on the general public is increasing. In the UK, for example, there is not simply the potential offered by video discs and new methods of information retrieval, but also that offered by the fourth television channel and cable television.

2.5 The role of intermediaries in humanities communication

2.5.1 *Learned societies*

The conference heard about the activities of the MLA and the

American Philological Association (APA), both of which were making great efforts on behalf of their users, although they operated on very different scales.

MLA members, for example, could search a structured database in their discipline and it was pointed out that an important aspect of the activities of learned societies was that their position allowed them to develop techniques specially tailored to their own disciplines, techniques which they could make available to their members and whose use they could monitor. The MLA also organised demonstrations, at which new technology and book displays were juxtaposed. Nineteen other learned societies used MLA facilities and the existence of this consortium allowed for reinvestment and for meaningful negotiations with the large database producers.

The APA was much smaller but feared the loss of autonomy which would occur if it joined the MLA. Nevertheless, the APA was engaged in an impressive range of activities such as setting priorities for filming, persuasion, exhortation, funding and educating members about developments in technology and in libraries.

An important aspect of the American scene is, of course, the ACLS which has no real parallel in the UK. Some of the British contingent found it difficult to imagine learned societies in their country acting in the ways they had just heard about and actually changing the way people work. They felt that the association with the university researcher was often not well-developed. But, to prevent themselves falling totally into envy and despondency, the UK contingent reminded the conference that *some* UK learned societies were very active and that *some* US ones *had* to be very backward!

As to the future, for all societies, but especially the smaller ones, money was the key restraint, but all agreed that learned societies should rethink their role — otherwise they would be bypassed. One important gap they could fill was to bring together interested groups to discuss the implications for their particular areas of the university cuts. Another was to interpose themselves between users and databases and act as intermediaries until the day dawns (if ever it does) when everyone is at home at a terminal. Many felt that the learned societies might stand a better chance of flourishing if they offered material benefits rather than simply 'spiritual' and supportive ones. But should societies involve themselves in database production? Some thought they should, since databases have potential for electronic communication and, by involving themselves in this, learned societies would be returning to their traditional and fundamental role as vehicles for informal communication. (There was then much discussion of the 'electronic college' and its implications — would demand for library services diminish as sources became more ownable by individuals, and would the concomitant reduction in shelf-browsing really matter?)

The discussion then widened. For example, it was asked if university presses could or should do any of the above. But the main direction the discussion then took was in relation to learned societies and the commercial sector. Should societies compete with commercial organisations? The MLA had experienced difficulty in obtaining the cooperation of commercial bodies in the organising of its demonstrations, even though, on a typical occasion, 8,000 educators might be present. But the conference thought that such demonstrations probably worked better anyway when individuals in the field brought along what they were doing, rather than commercial bodies being involved.

The discussion then broadened yet further into the relationship between the humanities as a whole and commercial interests. Some regretted the fact that there is comparatively little funding of humanities activities in the UK by commercial concerns, but others felt that humanists themselves were not always very adroit at laying hands on funds which might be available. They had allowed money to be diverted from them to the sciences and medicine, and it was essential that they improved their 'budget gamesmanship' by identifying and moving into areas where funds were available. One such area was, the conference thought, particularly important and that was the present emphasis on microcomputers which could, it was felt, be turned to the benefit of the humanities. The possibility was discussed of developing a database in the humanities for use on microcomputers by schoolchildren and undergraduates to help them appreciate the process of information retrieval.

2.5.2 Libraries

In the course of the conference so far, information had been exchanged on various initiatives and new projects involving libraries and humanists. It was reported, for example, that the CLR was involved in an experiment whereby 70 different sites, with online terminals connected to catalogues, were being monitored. Additionally, a major investment had been made in research and development to provide a computer link between text and records in California and the Library of Congress (LC).

However, from the John Rylands Library at the University of Manchester, the conference heard not of new projects taking off but of problems of survival, and of the threat posed to humanities research by the current economic situation. An agonising reappraisal of the academic role had taken place and many things — such as tenure, access to information — which had previously been accepted almost as rights were now being imperilled.

It was true that events had removed complacency and inefficency but cuts to staff and services had now gone beyond this level. At Manchester University Library, for example, out of a total staff of 175, 45 (of all grades) had to be lost. Support from the arts and social science faculties had been forthcoming — the library, after all, was their 'laboratory' — but other faculties were suspicious of the library. At Manchester, the cuts had meant a reduction in stock and services and the abandonment of plans for computerised catalogues. The depletion of the bookstock would have serious and permanent effects; the replacement of worn volumes had been restricted; fewer copies of undergraduate texts were being acquired; and the supply of reference tools was being restricted. Reductions in journal subscriptions had led to bad feelings between staff and users and attempts at special pleading. Feelings of resentment were rife. Student protesters adopted the slogan: 'Our library: no staff, no books, no use'.

But was this really affecting the quality and quantity of academic research in the humanities? It had to — since, even if humanities researchers could acquire the information needed for their research from sources other than their institutions' libraries, it remained the case that cutbacks in library budgets affected publishers' sales and hence the opportunities for academics to publish.

What solutions to these problems could the librarian seek? There were a number of candidates: greater efficiency; buying wisely and well and forgetting the pursuit of the ideal of the comprehensive collection; establishing a clearer notion of the back-up potential of libraries such as the British Library Lending Division and the British Library Reference Division; cooperation with other libraries (although this *could* cost more and achieve little); better methods of conservation (this was very important, the conference agreed); and full exploitation of the potential advantages of remote storage.

For this type of library, catering primarily for the academic researcher in the UK, tape and disc storage were probably going to be of little use in the near future for humanities material (although they might be for library services) and it was best to plan as if books would continue to be the main medium in the humanities for some time to come.

2.5.3 University presses

From the presentations given on this topic, it was clear that university presses both in the USA and the UK are operating in a state of perpetual crisis. At Princeton University Press, the conference was told, print runs were being reduced because the cuts meant that fewer books were being bought, costs were rising, and prices were rising. Potential solutions were: subsidies, reductions in royalties, and cheaper manufacturing methods. (On the last point, it was significant that typesetting for scholarly books constituted half of the manufacturing costs and that manufacturing costs constituted half the publishing costs.) Books were perceived as being expensive, but, on the whole, despite the fact that even a paperback could cost $19.50, they were not. Why should a book not cost the same as a good meal?

At Manchester University Press (MUP), the same vicious circle was in evidence — declining sales due to library cutbacks, escalating costs, rising prices, declining sales to individuals and institutions. Nevertheless, academic book prices had recently increased less than other book prices and less than the rate of inflation. The same possible solutions were also being examined. British university presses had tried to manage without subsidies, although, obviously, there was some form of subsidy from the university. At MUP, the university paid the interest on MUP's overdraft and subsidised its rents. Possible external sources of subsidy were the British Academy, philanthropic foundations and industry. On the whole, it was not as difficult for scholars to find funds for travel as for publication and it seemed sensible that when funding bodies allocated funds for research, they should also allocate funds for publishing.

As far as the humanities were concerned, there was little use of new technology in UK publishing, but, at MUP, efforts were being made to eliminate keyboarding by the use of authors' tapes and camera-ready copy. Tapes, however, were not without their problems — there were those of compatibility, for example, and many printers resisted them. Similarly, there was a resistance to camera-ready copy by academics, and electric typewriters were by no means universal. There had to be a move towards a climate of opinion whereby cheaper methods were acceptable and work was judged on its scholarly merit and not on the form and manner of its publication.

Part of the story of book prices, of course, involved the bookseller, who was not represented at the conference. It was noted, however, that booksellers are, on the whole, accepting new technology.

Two other possible strategies for dealing with the present difficulties were also discussed. One was giving books more appeal. But did this mean that university presses should go for bestsellers? This led on to a longer discussion of a topic briefly touched on before — the choice of potential titles and subjects by publishers. At MUP, every publishing decision was the result of a combination of economic and scholarly considerations. Particular subject strengths and decisions to move into new subject areas were linked to subject strengths within the university. Another strategy was to give more consideration to the *type* of book published. Three types were discussed — textbooks, research monographs and state of the art reviews (usually written by mature scholars). University presses were inevitably moving into the more lucrative textbook market — indeed some books which did not start their lives that way ended up as textbooks! Hard copy would continue to be the most useful format for textbooks, but new ways of publishing research monographs must become available. Research monographs were expensive to set, difficult to edit and had small sales. They undoubtedly caused the most problems for the university presses.

General discussion centred on possible methods of cheaper publication — such as paperbacks, microfiche and schemes like the data deposit scheme whereby extended supplementary material is obtainable separately from the main work to which it refers from the British Library Lending Division.

2.5.4 *Conclusions*

All agreed that this session had produced more problems than solutions and, certainly, answers to the questions posed as guidelines for the session (see Section 2.9) were barely glimpsed.

At times, the 'shadowy figure of the user' had scarcely made his presence felt. At others, he appeared almost as a puppet, manipulated by the intermediaries.

The problems facing academic publishing were traditional ones and trying to solve them by new technology might not always be appropriate. The end product of fewer titles was not necessarily a bad thing in itself. New technology might provide some answers for the libraries, bedevilled as they were by dwindling resources and increasing demand. Learned societies faced the challenge of re-establishing their role and choosing between diverse possible functions and diverse possible methods.

2.6 Discussion of conclusions

By this stage of the conference, it was clear that a massive area had been covered and some of it rather superficially. During this session, some of the points raised already were expanded and related to others in the hope that some consensus could be reached from which suggested solutions and recommendations might follow in the next (and final) session.

One point on which all agreed was that it was vital to have data about communication in the humanities. Despite pressure in the USA, nothing had been done to implement the recommendation in the National Enquiry that a clearing-house facility with this remit should be established. The Enquiry itself made erroneous assumptions because of lack of data. There was already a great deal of exchange of information and records between the USA and the UK, and it would be useful if a data-gathering facility similar to that envisaged for the USA could be set up in the UK.

The discussion returned to the theme of secondary versus primary material and which was the more problematic. Microfilm was most useful for some types of primary material. Although much had been done for primary material, there was still scope for improvement — for example, work needed to be done on the manipulation of text to allow, say, the structure of language to be examined. A new and important question was that of what exactly was available on machine-readable databases and Rutgers was said to be interested in this. Subject access was still undeveloped in the humanities and a report on this was to be published later in the year in the USA.

Information retrieval systems should be looked at carefully, since many were not user-friendly. Such systems should require the minimum alteration in habits. User-friendliness, however, cost money.

The development of databases should not be left to commercial enterprises — if profits were to be made, why should learned societies not make them?

Cooperation amongst intermediaries, such as the university presses and the smaller journals, should be encouraged. Consortia could save money and produce better services.

It was essential to bring the user into the debate. The Association of American Universities (AAU) and the CLR had supported a series of discussions with this intention, on topics such as the preservation of humanities material, shared collection development, the future of technology and bibliographic systems. It was thought to be advisable to tackle this problem at the local level and, although it was a good idea to aim at the senior scholar (for example, on the matter of camera-ready copy), he should not be too senior, since, it was felt, *very* senior scholars do not communicate!

There was some discussion on the interface between machines and the humanist. Here, perhaps, hope lay with the future — younger people can and do gain a sense of control by interacting with a machine and they see it not as a scientific or technical tool but as a means of creating.

This led on to discussion of the interfaces throughout the humanities communication system. Where friction existed — between users and providers, at times, for example — was this inevitable? The National Enquiry had very much been about this matter. Many present felt that if certain parts of the system were natural enemies of others, it was not a system *they* wanted to be part of! Perhaps, then, it was necessary to be very clear about whether aspects of the interfaces were as they were by nature, or through force of circumstance.

2.7 Summing up and recommendations

The final, summing-up session took place on the Monday morning. It was first necessary to make implicit what had become abundantly clear to all — the binational aspect of the conference had been a great success. It therefore seemed sensible that the recommendations would be framed with joint action in mind, not only to avoid unnecessary duplication, but also because unleashing the purse strings would mean more value for money if the work was coordinated with similar work being conducted in another country.

The findings of the conference fell under the following headings:

Data for decision

Up-to-date information on the processes and phenomena being discussed was lacking. The conference therefore endorsed previous recommendations that an Office for Scholarly Communication should be set up in the USA to collect and analyse data on communication in the humanities. An activity in the UK to parallel and liaise with this initiative was thought to be urgently required. Thought should be given to regular updates. In particular, further information on relevant American developments was needed in the UK and a visit by an appropriate person to observe and then report back on these developments was suggested.

Research

Further research into scholarly communication in the humanities was needed on both sides of the Atlantic and, if possible, it should be coordinated. It was imperative that such research should be supervised by a reasonably senior scholar with the research itself being carried out by a mix of humanities scholars and information specialists.

Education

An experimental Anglo-American summer school should be held to familiarise new researchers in the humanities with the applications of new technology to their work. There should, however, first be an investigation of the exact state of present provision in this area. In the case of more senior scholars, demonstrations were the most effective means of preaching to the unconverted. An experimental database should be set up to introduce students and others to information retrieval and the applications of new technology in the humanities. Personalised databases on microcomputers would become increasingly important and efforts should be made to influence their development in the humanities.

Other aspects of new technology

At least in the case of the UK, a mechanism was required for bridging the gap between the researchers and the developers of potentially relevant new technology. Most learned societies, the conference concluded, could and should do much more to help and advise researchers and to liaise with service providers on matters relating to new technology. New technololgy could be put to the service of 'old technology' in areas such as conservation, and hence the conference noted with approval the research programme on conservation supported by the BLR&D Department.

Humanities research and the general public

The link between humanities research and the general public needed further exploration and thought should be given to how the public image of humanities research could be improved.

There was a need for an international structure for humanities activities similar to that existing for the social sciences. The conference had started the process by establishing an informal network, an invisible college in scholarly communication in the humanities. Pending larger-scale developments, a clearing-house activity should be established — a short newsletter to alert humanities workers, social scientists, librarians, booksellers, publishers, etc. to developments in scholarly communication in the humanities.

The consensus was that the conference had been very successful, not only because of the interesting nature of the discussion, but also because the possibility of action being taken on the various recommendations was high. Moreover, the benefits which it had been hoped would be achieved as a result of the binational nature of the conference were fully realised. Further conferences of this nature (ideally involving scholars of other countries) should be considered.

2.8 'Communication in the humanities': list of participants

Roger S Bagnall	— Associate Professor of Classics and History, Columbia University and Secretary-Treasurer of the APA
Herbert S Bailey, Jr	— Director, Princeton University Press
John R Banks	— Editor, MUP
John Boardman	— Professor of Classical Art and Archaeology, Oxford University
David W Breneman	— Senior Fellow in Economical Studies, Brookings Institution
Warren J Haas	— President, CLR
Thomas E Hart	— Professor of Germanic Philology, Syracuse University
Sir Harry Hookway	— Chief Executive, British Library
Susan M Howley	— Project Officer, BLR&D Department
Jack Meadows	— Departmental Head, Astronomy and the History of Science, Leicester University and Project Head, Primary Communications Research Centre, Leicester University
Thomas A Noble	— Executive Associate, ACLS

Margaret O'Hare	— Section Head, BLR&D Department
Michael A Pegg	— Director, The John Rylands University Library of Manchester
Brian J Perry	— Acting Director*, BLR&D Department
Joseph Raben	— Professor of English, City University of New York and Editor of *Computers and the Humanities*
Hans Rütimann	— Deputy Executive Director, MLA
Glanmor Williams	— Professor of History, University College of Swansea

* Now Director

2.9 'Communication in the humanities': conference programme

Friday evening	(Chairman — Professor A J Meadows)
7 May	Administrative matters
Saturday morning 8 May	RETROSPECTIVE REVIEW OF RESEARCH INTO HUMANITIES COMMUNICATION
	(Chairman — Sir Harry Hookway Speakers — Dr DW Breneman — USA — Ms M O'Hare — UK)

1. What has been learnt from previous studies?
2. What have been the problems of implementing research findings?
3. To what extent have financial considerations hindered both the research and its implementation?
4. Have there been difficulties in finding qualified research personnel and interested institutions?

| *Saturday afternoon* | THE PROBLEMS OF RESEARCH WORKERS IN THE HUMANITIES AS ORIGINATORS AND USERS OF INFORMATION |
| | (Chairman — Professor TE Hart Speakers — Professor J Raben — USA — Professor G Williams — UK) |

1. Do these problems relate to a knowledge of sources?
2. What difficulties relate to access (availability of material, need for travel, etc.)?
3. What are the financial problems involved?
4. What will be the effects of new information technology?
5. Do humanities researchers have a sufficient knowledge of other research and research workers in their own field?
6. Is resistance to change still a significant factor? If so, is it a good or bad thing?

Saturday evening

THE DISSEMINATION OF HUMANITIES RESEARCH TO A WIDER AUDIENCE

(Chairman — Mr TA Noble
Speakers — Mr WJ Haas — USA
— Professor AJ Meadows — UK)

1. What problems does the passage of information from research workers to non-researchers raise?
2. What should be the roles of (i) text books, (ii) school-teachers, (iii) review journals (weeklies, etc.), (iv) radio and television in the dissemination of humanities research to a wider audience?
3. Will databases for personal computers become important?

Sunday morning
9 May

THE ROLE OF THE INTERMEDIARIES IN HUMANITIES COMMUNICATION

(Chairman — Professor J Boardman
Speakers — Professor RS Bagnall — USA
— Mr HS Bailey, Jr — USA
— Mr JR Banks — UK
— Dr MA Pegg — UK)

1. For all members of this group, how important are financial restrictions on their activities?

2. For learned societies, what problems are raised by their publishing activities? What points need to be considered concerning their informal communication activities (e.g. conferences)?

3. For publishers, what particular problems does humanities publishing raise? Where do university presses fit into the picture?

4. For libraries and archives, what problems are presented by storage and access requirements? What is the role of new technology? What are the current and future prospects for acquisitions? What are the problems of conservation?

Sunday afternoon

DISCUSSION OF CONCLUSIONS
(Chairman — Mr H Rütimann)

This may be structured round the groupings employed in previous sessions (researchers, societies, etc.) and the lines of communication between them. In the light of the previous discussions, this session should try to define areas in humanities communication where further activity (collection and/or dissemination of information, research, etc.) might be useful. The main emphasis will continue to be on activities of significance in the Anglo-American context.

Monday morning
10 May

SUMMING UP AND RECOMMEND-
ATIONS

(Chairman — Mr BJ Perry)

3 Recent developments in communication in the humanities in the USA: report by Dr M Katzen on a study visit to the USA, October-November 1982

Introduction

This report is the outcome of a study visit by the author to the USA in October-November 1982, which was commissioned by the BLR&D Department as a result of the recommendation of the Cawthorpe House conference that more information on the American situation was required in the UK. The aims of the visit were to identify recent developments in research communication in the humanities in the USA (including the use of new technologies) and to investigate possible areas of Anglo-American collaboration in this field. The report also draws on information gathered during a previous study visit to the USA, with essentially similar objectives, undertaken in June 1979. During the course of these visits, extensive interviews were conducted with members of funding agencies, learned societies and libraries, with university press directors and members of other publishing organisations, with specialists in information and communication, and with research workers in the humanities. The author wishes to record her grateful thanks to all those interviewed, who generously provided so much useful information, and to the BLR&D Department for funding these visits. Although every effort has been made to make this report as objective as possible, the views expressed are necessarily the result of the author's impressions gained during the course of these visits, and from follow-up telephone interviews conducted between December 1982 and November 1983.

3.1 Initiatives of the late 1970s

Within the last decade, there has been a considerable amount of discussion and activity concerned with the humanities in the USA. One important aspect of this concern was 'a profound disquiet about the state of the humanites in our culture', to quote the opening sentence of the report of the Commission on the Humanities appointed by the Rockefeller Foundation in 1978 to assess 'the humanities' place and prospects'. Its lucid and eloquent report, published in 1980, emphasised (and called upon educators to emphasise):

the value of the humanities for effective self-expression; for enjoyment and judgment of the arts; for understanding other cultures, and for assessment of ethical problems, issues of public policy and questions of value raised by science and technology[1].

The Commission recognised and stressed the intimate connection between the value placed upon the humanities in American life and the importance accorded to these disciplines in the educational system, starting with the curricula offered in the school system and continuing into undergraduate and postgraduate programmes in colleges and universities in the USA. In several places in its report, the Commission noted that the erosion of humanistic studies in the USA had, to a large extent, gone hand in hand with the increasing pressure of more straitened circumstances in the economy as a whole in the 1970s, when inflation and unemployment succeeded the expansion of the 1960s. It was also partly attributable to the effect of long-term demographic trends in reducing enrolments at all levels in the educational system, especially in higher education:

> The experience of the last three decades has clearly shown that the fortunes of the humanities, higher education and our culture are closely interwoven. The prosperity in higher education in the 1950's and 1960's, itself a reflection of our nation's material and technical progress, was in some respects a boon for the humanities. The economic stringencies and re-appraisals of the 1970's and the consequent re-assessment of higher education will inevitably test the strength of the humanities[2].

The appointment of the Humanities Commission was an outstanding example, among many others, of a resilient energy in the face of danger that was displayed in the later 1970s and was directed to finding ways of strengthening and vitalising the humanities. Thus, for example, this period saw the formation of two new national organisations, the Community College Humanities Association and the American Association for the Advancement of the Humanities (AAAH). The AAAH was founded in 1978, partly along the lines of the American Association for the Advancement of Science, to serve as a forum for discussing matters concerning the humanities disciplines and their interconnections, through its annual conference and its newsletter, as well as to form a bridge between the humanities and the general public and to act as a pressure group. It has recently ceased to function owing to lack of support, in part because of an insufficiently defined role. In 1981, another smaller, but more focused effort — the National Humanities Alliance (NHA) — sprang up, to provide a spokesman for the humanities in the political world of Washington.

During the same period, the National Humanities Center was established near Chapel Hill, North Carolina, with support from several foundations, along the lines of the Institute for Advanced Study at Princeton, to provide fellowships for outstanding scholars to spend some time there (normally a year), pursuing their research, and to hold advanced seminars, which are later published, on themes relevant to the humanities. More recently, in 1981, in order to help attract outstanding teachers and scholars into graduate research in the humanities and to help sustain leading graduate schools, the Andrew W Mellon Foundation announced that it would spend some $24 million over the following 10 years on a programme of graduate fellowships covering such fields as English and comparative literature, American studies, history, foreign languages and literatures, the classics, archaeology, linguistics, philosophy, art, history, religion, musicology and area studies[3]. The programme is intended to help counteract the decline in the quality of applicants to leading graduate schools, which has come about as a result of the stagnant state of employment opportunities in higher education for new PhDs in the humanities, and which has meant, in some cases, a decline in the scope and range of graduate programmes offered, even in leading graduate schools. The NEH has funded several investigations into such matters as tenure practices in four-year colleges, the scale and pattern of doctorates awarded, employment opportunities for humanities PhDs, the nature of the Master's degree and of undergraduate programmes, and current sources of funding for the humanities in academic institutions, in order to monitor trends in universities and colleges.

Efforts to provide some additional means of financial support to research and scholarship in the humanities point to a realisation by both private and public funding agencies that the vitality of the humanities in education and as a force in American culture must ultimately depend on the ability of scholars in the humanistic disciplines to continue to carry on their research work and to advance the frontiers of knowledge in these fields. Unless a strong and vigorous research effort continues to take place, sterility and inanition will supervene. Conversely, unlike those branches of learning in science and technology and in the social sciences, which are more broadly based in industry and the professions, as well as in academic institutions, research in the humanities is almost exclusively carried on by scholars attached to universities and colleges. Thus the combined effects of recession and inflation, as well as of falling numbers of enrolments in institutions of higher learning, have borne heavily on the system of scholarly communication in the humanities which underpins the conduct and flow of scholarly research. The erosion of the budgets of American academic and research libraries has meant reduction in the purchases of journals and particularly of monographs in the humanities. Resource sharing among libraries and the fall in the number of individual purchases of books and journals in the face of ever-rising costs of production and distribution have put increasing pressure on the viability of scholarly publishing in the humanities, especially the operations of university presses which are faced with a falling level of support from their parent institutions.

Although difficulties in communication are more acute for the humanities than for other branches of learning, they reflect many of the problems of information transfer in general in the USA. During the 1960s, but especially in the 1970s, a great deal of time and effort was expended in the USA on suggesting methods to improve the information system as a whole, particularly in relation to library and information services. During the later 1970s, the idea gained ground that there should be a national information policy for the country, to be carried out by a new national library agency, specifically responsible for its formulation and implementation. One key element in this policy was the proposal to establish a National Periodicals Center, which would store and distribute less-used periodicals, and thereby reduce the heavy burden of inter-library lending on the major research and public libraries. Another was the establishment of a comprehensive national bibliographic system, which would enhance the flow of bibliographic information both nationally and internationally.

The report of the National Enquiry into Scholarly Communication, published in 1979, placed the communication problems of the humanities within the context of this debate, by endorsing those proposals aimed at improving access and retrieval of information in general (which would necessarily also improve humanities communication) as well as by tackling the specific problems affecting the publication of research in the humanities. The National Enquiry constitutes a real landmark in this field for a number of reasons. It was the first major research investigation of its kind, a three-year project funded to the tune of $600,000 by a combination of public and private funds granted by the NEH and the Rockefeller, Ford and Mellon Foundations, under the sponsorship of the influential ACLS. Its report emphasised that:

> The various constituencies involved in scholarly communication — the scholars themselves, the publishers of books and of learned journals, the research librarians, the learned societies — are all components of a single system, and are thus fundamentally dependent upon each other. Moreover, this single system in all its parts is highly sensitive to influence from two outside factors — the

actions of the funding agencies and the development of new technologies[4].

Its recommendations were, therefore, directed mainly at improving the system as a whole, through qualitative rather than quantitative changes. The Enquiry recognised that the communication system needed outside financial support from both public and private funding agencies, but it also considered measures of self-help, mainly by publishers.

Its 12 main recommendations are worth summarising briefly here, since they have already influenced thinking about scholarly communication in the humanities, and will doubtless continue to do so in the future. The National Enquiry supported the creation of a national bibliographic system, a national periodicals centre and a national library agency, urged librarians and publishers to cooperate with the Copyright Clearance Center, and emphasised the need to control the net growth of humanities journals. It pointed to the advantages of economies of scale in publishing, recommending that small journals use the services of larger established organisations for production, subscription fulfilment and so on, and that university presses establish collaborative fulfilment centres for order processing, warehousing and shipping and take vigorous steps to expand overseas markets. It called on universities without presses to share the financial burden of publishing with existing university presses by sponsorship and other means. It urged foundations to broaden their role *vis-à-vis* humanities communication, by financing system-wide improvements, encouraging collaboration among publishers and granting title subsidies. Finally, it recommended that an Office for Scholarly Communication be established within the NEH to monitor developments in the system, and that the ACLS, the Association of American University Presses (AAUP) and the Association of Research Libraries (ARL) form a standing committee to discuss and direct technological change. Although not all its recommendations have come to fruition, many of the initiatives that have been taken in the last few years accord with the views expressed in its report — at times almost coincidentally.

3.2 Altered perspectives in the early 1980s

Seen from the perspective of the early 1980s, the later 1970s were a period of vigorous activity in the formulation of large-scale strategic plans to improve information transfer in all fields, including the humanities. These were years in which the manifestation of long-term structural changes in the communication system — notably those caused by the continuing effects of the expansion of research in the

1960s, experienced as an 'information explosion', and of declining enrolments in higher education, combined with the more immediate difficulties of the beginnings of inflation and recession — evoked a sense of crisis which stimulated a search for grand, national solutions, many of which were predicated upon federal action and financial support.

The atmosphere of the first quarter of the 1980s strikes an outside observer as being rather different. It is less dramatic, more sober and more modest. It is perhaps not too much to say that, although there is a considerable amount of activity in various directions, it is being conducted more quietly, with less fanfare than before, partly though not entirely, because much of it is concerned with the implementation rather than the formulation of plans. In some areas, however, although the goals remain unchanged, they are being approached rather differently. For example, the emphasis on creating new centralised national agencies — such as the national library agency and the national periodicals centre, both of which have been shelved — has been replaced by efforts to direct and coordinate the activities of existing agencies towards common goals of improvement in library and information services. The emphasis on distributed rather than centralised effort, is, of course, in accord with traditional American thinking, and is partly a matter of changed perspective, one that developments in computer technology and their applications to such matters as library networking and cataloguing have made more feasible.

3.2.1 More limited federal involvement

One important pointer to the change of mood in the USA during the last few years is the altered attitude towards the role of government, particularly the federal government, in relation to the dissemination of information. There has always been a certain tension in American thought between conflicting notions of the desirability, or otherwise, of active government involvement in this field. This tension remains, but there has been a distinct shift in the balance of opinion in the past few years. In the later 1970s, there was widespread, though not universal, support in some circles for the notion that public agencies should take the initiative in investing in system-wide improvements that were to be seen as a form of overhead social capital, although, wherever possible, market forces should be allowed to run their course. But, as witnessed by the report of the Task Force appointed by the National Commission on Libraries and Information Science to make recommendations on public/private sector interaction in providing information services, the opinion now prevails that the private sector should be left free to provide all the information services it can, with the role of government virtually reduced merely to facilitating this process[5].

This shift of opinion is attributable partly to the change in administration in the USA and partly to the effects of the recession. The immediate consequence has been that the budgets of some federal funding agencies, including the National Commission on Libraries and Information Science and the NEH, have been reduced, which presumably must mean an increasing reliance upon funding by private foundations, such as the Andrew W Mellon Foundation and others, which have already played a vital role in financing projects to improve scholarly communication. However, in spite of the more austere financial conditions of the past few years, there have recently been a number of important initiatives in the USA designed to improve research communication in the humanities, many of which are concerned with the application of new technologies to information transfer.

3.2.2   The impact of computers

Over the past several years, there has been a rather rapid and significant penetration of computers into the world of scholarship. This has been most evident in science and technology and in the social sciences, where online database searching is coming to be taken for granted as a method of information retrieval, and where word processors are increasingly used by authors to prepare material for publication. Matters are by no means so far advanced in the humanities, even though there has long been a growing band of humanities scholars interested in using computers in their research work. This interest is evidenced by *Computers and the Humanities*, a quarterly journal which has existed since 1966, and which publishes a biannual *Directory of scholars* active in this field; in January 1983, its editor, Joseph Raben, began to publish a bimonthly newsletter, *SCOPE* (Scholarly Communication Online Publishing and Education), available both in printed form and via BITnet and other online networks. Nevertheless, the majority of humanities scholars remained uninfluenced by these trends. In the last year or two, however, the erstwhile ignorance of, and resistance to, the potentialities of electronic equipment are beginning to give way, rather suddenly it seems, to a virtual explosion of interest in the application of new technologies to the dissemination of information.

The main reason is the proliferation of microcomputers in all aspects of life in the USA, with a rapid saturation of the mass market reminiscent of the spread of television in the 1950s. Children now learn to use computers at school and they and their families play computer games. There has been an enormous increase in the ownership of cheap and relatively user-friendly personal computers, such as the Apple and the Tandy TRS, and word processing has spread from offices to homes.

The take-up of computers by the public at large is now beginning to affect scholars in the humanities. The experience of the MLA provides a striking example of this phenomenon. For a number of years, it has made its annual bibliography available online, on Lockheed's DIALOG since 1978 and on BRS since 1982, persevering in the face of scepticism, or, at best, merely token interest on the part of its membership. But at last it can report that its persistence has been rewarded. There are now over 1,000 online searches a month of the *MLA international bibliography* and the receipts from online searching constitute a significant and growing proportion of its income. In the last year or so, the MLA has been so impressed by the number of queries it has received on the applications of new technologies to information transfer, that it has decided to issue a new series of publications entitled *Technology and the Humanities,* aimed at the uninitiated, on various electronic devices, including word processors and video discs, as well as the use of computers in teaching and research. Starting in 1983, the MLA Annual Convention will include an Electronic Workshop, a forum for scholars who have developed computer applications such as computer-aided instruction software, bibliography formatting programs, databases, video discs and administrative software.

It would seem that the USA is in the midst of an academic revolution which will result in computers becoming as widespread on campuses as photocopiers. Online catalogues are increasingly used in academic and research libraries, and user acceptance is growing. Computer literacy is now beginning to be regarded as an essential part of a balanced curriculum, mainly at present in the sciences, social sciences and in some professional fields, but also increasingly in the humanities. After many years of pioneering effort by enthusiasts like John Kemeny, President of Dartmouth College, many other colleges and universities including, for example, Harvard, now insist that all humanities undergraduates take at least one course on computers as a requirement for a degree. Other institutions have gone further. Carnegie-Mellon University now has a hard-wired campus with 4,500 terminal outlets; it has signed an agreement with IBM to develop an interconnected campus network of personal computers for staff, faculty and students; and all its students are required to bring their own personal computers with them when they enter college. Stanford

University will be introducing this requirement for its 1984 entering class and will be operating its own system of electronic mail. IBM has supplied 125 personal computers to this institution and they will be linked by telephone to the Stanford University Library and the Research Libraries Group (RLG) network. A recent survey showed that 25% of Stanford's staff and faculty have small computers and terminals at home, and that 60% expected to do a significant part of their work at home in five years' time, using campus-linked home computers for text editing and printing; accessing online library catalogues; accessing, storing and manipulating data; and message transmission. Again, since 1982, all freshmen at Stevens Institute of Technology who wish to major in science or systems planning and management must own personal computers. At Clarkson College of Technology, all freshmen entering in the fall of 1983 were issued with Zenith Z-100 desk top computers[6]. The University of Michigan Library is planning to install terminals in the offices of the faculties of English and history, which will provide direct access to the machine-readable catalogues, and the School of Library Science there is developing programs for personal computers so that scholars can transfer records from large databases and reformat them to compile bibliographies[7]. As these examples show, it is mainly some of the technologically orientated colleges and universities that are trying to ensure that computers are used by students as a matter of routine. But the trend will surely spread, as evidenced by the almost unanimous agreement on the need for computer literacy at a recent national Educom meeting.

The issues facing scholarly communication in the 1980s have been cogently summed up by Warren J Haas, President of the CLR, a body which is taking a leading role in improving library and information services in the USA. In a major recent review of computing in documentation and scholarly research, he wrote:

> After years (some would say generations) of stability, scholarly communication is now in a period of extensive change. All organisational components and all processes are involved. The driving forces, for the most part, are not new; rather they are old problems amplified by severe economic difficulties and technological prospects[8].

He continues:

> Transformation of the system, organisationally and functionally, is seen by many as essential if capabilities are to be maintained and costs controlled. The application of computer and communications technology is considered, rightly or wrongly, as the means to that end[9].

3.3 Consultation between constituents of the communication system

The transformation of the system has many implications, as yet unexplored, for the way in which scholars in the humanities will conduct their research. As the National Enquiry's report stressed, the communication system consists of a series of interlocking and interdependent parts, and changes in one part of the system may well have repercussions on the smooth and efficient working of other parts. The National Enquiry therefore urged the necessity of 'markedly increased consultation among the leaders in the various components and influences' of the system, and called for the creation of a standing committee, drawn from learned societies, research libraries and university presses, which would discuss the nature and direction of technological change, and be able to advise on the best method of introducing and implementing that change. Such a committee, the Committee on Scholarly Communication, was set up in 1980 under the aegis of the ACLS, the ARL and the AAUP by a grant from the Carnegie Corporation. The Committee has now begun to formulate plans for the establishment of an independent research centre, provisionally called the Office of Scholarly Communication and Technology which, it is to be hoped, would be funded by grants from private foundations and the NEH (*vide,* Chapter 5). If these plans materialise, the new Office will provide a mechanism to monitor the rate and direction of changes in the system of scholarly communication, and its research will help to ensure that technological innovation promotes, rather than hinders, scholarly activity.

Another major recent instance of consultation between representatives of different constituencies with an interest in information transfer, which is likely to have important consequences for the future, is a series of meetings between university administrators, research librarians and scholars to discuss the problems of research libraries. The meetings were arranged jointly by the ACLS, the AAU and the CLR.

At an initial meeting in 1980, five main topic areas were identified for detailed study: bibliographical systems, preservation, resource sharing, technology and research librarianship. Five task forces were appointed to study these areas and reported a year later. From their detailed recommendations, four main common threads emerged which underlined the need for continuing close consultation between learned societies, university administrators, librarians, publishers and funding agencies:

> that cooperation was the appropriate means to several ends but that existing structures for cooperation were inadequate;

that existing funding patterns were institutionally centred and a constraint on making fundamental changes in the system;

that computer communication and text storage technologies offered prospects for improved service and cost control but capital costs were high and sources of funds few;

that the effects of some changes were far reaching; faculty members and representatives of key disciplines must participate in setting the course and promoting understanding amongst their colleagues [10].

Growing out of the work of these task forces, a conference on research libraries was held in December 1982 at Wingspread, Wisconsin, including university officers, faculty members, librarians and foundation officials. It identified a number of items for action and suggested establishing a continuing forum drawn from scholars, research libraries, publishing and universities to analyse major issues, monitor progress and marshal support for libraries [11]. In consequence, in October 1983, Forum II, a meeting comprising representatives of all these constituencies was held at Wye Plantation, Maryland, to discuss the national and regional aspects of collecting and preserving library materials. Further meetings on other topics will be held in due course.

3.4 Attempts to improve system performance

The foregoing section has been mainly concerned with the results of a number of discussions, investigations and research projects into different aspects of communication in the USA, aimed at improving the performance of various parts of the system. Some efforts have been directed to information transfer generally, in all disciplines; others have focused on matters specifically related to the humanities. A considerable number of initiatives have been undertaken in recent years by libraries, learned societies and publishers, varying from large-scale cooperative ventures, mainly related to libraries and information services, to more modest and restricted ventures on the part of the learned societies and university presses. The majority of these efforts have been funded by public and private foundations which, for many years, have been very active in providing the necessary support. It is not possible to discuss all these initiatives in detail. Rather, an attempt will be made to give a sense of the direction in which things are moving in the USA by describing some of the projects, recently completed or under way at present, in three main categories: access to information, provision of research resources and dissemination of research results.

3.4.1 Access to information

The most far-reaching and comprehensive programme to improve the means for users to gain access to information is being conducted under the aegis of the CLR, a body which has played a pre-eminent role in mobilising and coordinating funding for library projects by public and private foundations. A major manifestation of its efforts is its Bibliographic Service Development Program (BSDP). The BSDP started in 1978 as a five-year programme with funding now completed at some $6.3 million from the NEH and seven private foundations. It comprises a group of inter-related projects directed to the implementation of a national computer-based bibliographic network, by coordinating the activities of major producers of bibliographic records, and by assisting in the creation of common standards of record content and format, and of operating procedures. Many of the most important projects to improve access to information have been conducted under the umbrella of the BSDP.

One of these is a series of projects aimed at creating common standards for the content and organisation of bibliographic records, including the application of cataloguing rules for cataloguing machine-readable data files, the standardisation of institution identifiers and holdings statements, and a system for recording and communicating cancellation of serials. In this connection, it should be noted that the RLG is undertaking a project funded by the Ford and Mellon Foundations and the NEH to incorporate Chinese, Japanese and Korean vernacular script into primary bibliographic files.

Another series of projects undertaken under the aegis of the BSDP is designed to facilitate the inter-linking of computer systems to enable users to locate bibliographic information in other systems. The most recent of these is a series of grants to RLG, the Washington Library Network (WLN) and the LC to develop a Standard Network Interconnection, to enable their computer systems to communicate by developing telecommunication protocols for sharing information between a diversity of computer systems. The implication of this work is that, eventually, any computer system will be able to connect with any other computer system to create a nationwide bibliographic database.

The same three institutions (LC, RLG and WLN) have also been developing a name authority file, that is a thesaurus or dictionary of standard acceptable forms for personal and corporate names, which will form the basis of a name authority file service which they will maintain and develop. The use of this service by other libraries will mean that eventually there will be created a comprehensive, national, non-redundant, bibliographic database, prospectively and retrospectively.

Work is also under way on the much more difficult task of creating a comparable subject authority file. This will enable users to make more precise literature searches, especially of monographs in the humanities and social sciences. One step in this direction was an analysis of indexing in art and architecture, funded by the NEH, which clarified some of the more general problems involved in subject indexing.

The CLR has also initiated a series of investigations into online library catalogue use. The main aim was to evaluate the performance of different types of online catalogue in academic and public libraries which provide direct access to users. The project was designed to gauge how acceptable online catalogues are to different types of users, and to highlight any difficulties in using them, in order to establish guidelines that will promote both satisfactory performance and economical operation. (It is interesting to note that this study underlined the importance of subject searching by users.) In addition, one college has been given funding to hold annual meetings of faculty and library staff on the effects of library computerisation on users and use.

The CLR has also funded a project at Rutgers University for the bibliographic control of machine-readable texts in the humanities, with a view to creating a national authority file for these records[12].

A new CLR programme concerned with information delivery services is just getting under way. As with the BSDP, it will concentrate on fact finding, promotion of coordinated effort, and extended consultation with university officers and the scholarly world.

Analogous work has been directed to coordinating and interlocking efforts related to the bibliographic control of manuscript material, under the leadership of the LC. One aspect of this work relates to the interchange of information between manuscript repositories, archives and record centres, and has been undertaken by the National Information Systems Task Force of the Society of American Archivists. The Task Force has been constructing a standardised data element dictionary, defining a format for the exchange of data between institutions, especially in machine-readable form, exploring models for inter-institutional networks, and defining the functional requirements of a total information system within an archive, record centre or manuscript repository. As in the case of the activities related to the national bibliographic system, the aim is not so much to impose a standardised procedure on the internal management of collections as to create the means to facilitate the exchange of information between different systems[13].

3.4.2 Provision of research resources

Scholarship in all fields, but especially in the humanities, depends on the availability of textual materials of all kinds. There is a great deal of activity in the USA related both to the preservation of material in existing collections, and to the provision of new documentary resources for scholarship — reference works, new editions, bibliographies and the like.

Conservation

In the last few years, there has been mounting concern among librarians and scholars alike over the deterioration of printed documents in American library collections, particularly those printed on acid paper over the last century. The LC, in a Statement on Paper Durability, has calculated that books printed on acid paper will take only between 25 and 50 years to deteriorate. Hence efforts are proceeding in two directions, to preserve existing collections and to try to ensure that new printed materials conform to standards in paper quality and binding which will prevent deterioration.

As far as preservation is concerned, up and down the country libraries are beginning to come to grips with the enormous problem of their deteriorating holdings. The main focus is on materials printed in the period 1880-1920, when standards of paper quality were very poor. The LC is leading the way with its own massive preservation programme, but many of the major libraries are also beginning to set up preservation units to de-acidify acid paper and to train preservation specialists. These procedures are very costly, hence an alternative strategy is to try to film those materials at risk, so that in any particular region or network, there will be at least one copy available, thus allowing duplicates to be discarded.

As one example of the kind of activity taking place that is particularly pertinent to the requirements of scholars, including those in the humanities, the RLG received a grant of $143,000 in October 1982 from the NEH to develop an RLG automated union list of microform master negatives. Ten members of RLG will enter such records into the Research Libraries Information Network databases. Such action will prevent duplicate filming among members of RLG and lay the basis for a cooperative preservation microfilming programme. A feature of the plan is the provision of a union list of microform master negatives, which will include also records on firm decisions to film[14]. In May 1983, the RLG received a three-year grant of $200,000 outright and up to $475,000 in matching grants from the NEH for a cooperative microfilming project of printed Americana from 1875 to 1900, involving some 30,000 American imprints. This is the first consortial arrangement of its kind, and will involve setting mutually agreed priorities on what to film, by the seven libraries concerned, all of which have substantial collections of Americana.

It will be noted that, as in the case of bibliographic activity, preservation initiatives are being taken on a cooperative rather than a centralised basis. It is interesting that in some instances there has been an attempt to take decisions on the strategies to be adopted with regard to preservation by librarians acting in conjunction with scholars. This was the case at Columbia University, where a committee of classicists was formed to consider preservation priorities with regard to scholarly materials pertinent to research in that field held by Columbia University Library, but, in the event, the effort proved too costly to pursue.

Over the past few years, efforts have been made to interest publishers and paper manufacturers in adhering to guidelines on book paper. The CLR established a Committee on Production Guidelines for Book Longevity in 1979, which drafted an interim report on book paper in 1981. It recommended *inter alia* that priorities be established for which types of scholarly material should be printed on acid-free paper and that such books be issued with an appropriate statement to that effect. The CLR also issued a preliminary report providing similar guidelines on binding methods in 1982[15]. The American National Standards Committee is in the process of drafting a national standard on paper quality.

New research tools

It is likely that more effort and funds are expended in the USA on creating new research resources and research tools for the humanities than in any other country in the world. The scale, range and variety of this central scholarly activity is truly impressive and spans the whole gamut of disciplines within the humanities. The reasons are not far to seek — the large number of universities and colleges in the USA, the emphasis on research and publication as a means of career advancement for faculty members in the humanities, as in the sciences and social sciences, and the existence of active learned societies, large and small, in all fields.

The role of funding agencies

However, there can be no doubt that funding agencies play an important, even a vital, role in sustaining and underpinning this type of scholarly endeavour. The aids to research which are produced — compilations, authoritative editions of major works, concordances, dictionaries, specialised bibliographies and the like — are in themselves works of scholarship and can be very time-consuming and expensive. In this context, the existence of a separate public funding agency, (the NEH), specifically devoted to channelling federal funds to support a variety of different types of projects in the humanities, including those related to research materials and research resources, is undoubtedly important, both as a source of funds, and also as a public endorsement of the value placed on these activities in the USA. It has been argued[16] recently that the humanities, by being placed under the responsibility of a separate funding agency, are thereby undervalued in comparison with science and technology and the social sciences, and that there should be one single research agency to deal with all branches of knowledge. It is true that the funds available to the NEH are much smaller than those granted to the National Science Foundation. The NEH's budget for 1982 was $130.6 million (though this sum represented a 14% reduction on the 1981 budget, it was nevertheless a vast improvement over the proposed cut of 44%). Of this, $15.7 million was allocated to research, including $6.0 million to research materials (research tools, such as dictionaries, encyclopaedias and databases; editions; translations and subventions for publication) and $3.4 million to research resources (including inventories, catalogues and bibliographies). These sums may, perhaps, seem comparatively modest, but the NEH now sees its role, as a federal agency in a time of budget restraint, as being a modest, limited one, though one that seeks to encourage and 'support the essential and the exemplary'[17]. By doing so, it can be thought of as to some extent providing an example for private foundations. Its system of 'matching grants', that is making a dollar for dollar contribution (or in the case of Challenge grants, one for every three dollars) to funds obtained from private sources, illustrates the concrete application of this principle. In point of fact, research in the humanities in the USA can draw on a multiplicity of funding agencies; many of the larger projects (for example, the National Enquiry) have received funds from several sources, so that the financial burden has been shared. One example is the very large database project being undertaken by the

Department of Romance Languages and Literatures at the University of Chicago. The Department has received a collection of 1,500 French texts, spanning the 18th to the 20th centuries, stored on magnetic tapes, from the Institut National de la Langue Française in Nancy, which became accessible online throughout North America in 1983. This project received a small planning grant from the NEH, but obtained its major funding from other sources.

Computer-based projects

Foundations have played a particularly important role in providing assistance for very large projects, especially those in which computerised methods are used. Using computers for the production of research tools and research resources can involve a great deal of expense, but often considerably shortens the time needed to complete them. The resulting machine-readable record can not only be output in a variety of formats and media but also enables the online text to be manipulated more easily, particularly if full advantage is taken of the resources of the computer to provide the depth of indexing required. For some years now, the NEH has encouraged the use of computerised methods (where they seemed appropriate) for the compilation of a variety of research tools and reference works and the advantages of computerisation have come to be more widely appreciated by research workers and other funding agencies alike. As Farr pointed out in a recent article:

> For certain types of classic research tools, the computer has literally transformed conventional assumptions and methodologies. In so doing, it has altered irrevocably the manner in which bibliographies, concordances, atlases and dictionaries are compiled and disseminated[18].

It would be impossible to detail all the projects of this kind being undertaken in the USA at present. There are a large number already, and interest in this type of research activity has increased considerably, as witnessed by the steady growth of the Association for Computers in the Humanities. All the signs indicate that computers will be used increasingly in the future. Indeed, they are almost indispensable for compiling certain types of research tools, particularly very large databases, concordances and lexicons, as well as research materials which should be brought out speedily and regularly (e.g. bibliographies) or be frequently updated (e.g. encyclopaedias).

To illustrate the sort of project that is being undertaken at present, the following examples may be cited:

the *Thesaurus linguae Graecae,* a very large database which will include some 90 million words comprising classical Greek texts from Homer to AD 600, being undertaken at the University of California at Irvine. Several concordances have already been produced from this database;

the *Dictionary of American regional English,* edited at the University of Wisconsin, which documents the occurrence of some 5 million words and idioms by region, and by various social indicators, thus enabling word usage to be mapped accordingly;

the *Dictionary of the Old Spanish language,* based on 13th century Spanish texts, being compiled at the University of Wisconsin, Madison;

The eighteenth century short title catalogue, a joint endeavour of Louisiana State University, the American Antiquarian Society, the British Library and 240 contributing libraries, which aims to identify all texts printed in Great Britain and its colonies in any language, and all texts printed in English elsewhere in the world from 1701 to 1800;

the continuing revision of the Wing *Short title catalogue of books printed in England, Scotland, Ireland and Wales, and British America, and of English books printed in other countries from 1641-1700,* directed from the Yale University Library and the MLA;

the Historical Boundary Datafile project, directed from the Newberry Library in Chicago, that is producing a cartographic database of boundary changes and a variety of statistical data covering all the territories, states and counties in the USA since 1788[19];

the *Annual international bibliography* of the MLA dealing with modern languages, literatures, linguistics and folklore, which, since the later 1970s, has been produced in-house by the MLA's own text-processing facilities, resulting in great savings of time and expense in producing the printed version. The bibliography is also available online, and the MLA has developed a sophisticated indexing system, the Contextual Indexing and Faceted Taxonomic Access System (CIFT) which provides a variety of access points for searching the database, including literary genres, themes, approaches, literary schools, literary movements and so on. The MLA has recently received a grant from the Mellon Foundation to produce a thesaurus of linguistic, literary and folklore terms. From the master file of journals indexed by the *International bibliography,* the MLA has produced a printed *MLA directory of periodicals,* which will be updated every two years, containing such details as editorial descriptions, subscription information and submission requirements[20]. At present the MLA is creating the

Book Review Editors On-line Data Base of journals in 25 disciplines that review university press and scholarly books. It will contain information about the likely subject coverage of books reviewed by each journal.

3.4.3 Problems of dissemination

One of the most intractable and critically important problems in the communication of research in the humanities is the dissemination of completed research to the scholarly community via publication. As the National Enquiry pointed out, 'much of the value or purpose of research is lost if others are not made aware of it'[21]. In the USA, as in the rest of the world, there are often acute difficulties in publishing the results of specialised research in the humanities. This has been especially true in the last five years or so, when publishers have been faced with rising editorial, production, marketing and distribution costs at a time when effective demand from libraries and individual purchasers is shrinking. The difficulties are especially evident in the case of specialised bibliographies emanating from small learned societies, small specialised humanities journals, and specialised monographs, all of which have limited sales, so that the unit cost of production is very high. In addition, many small learned publishers often lack professional expertise and management skills. In the USA, as elsewhere, there is an evident need to provide advisory and consultative services for current management, and to provide training for graduates to prepare them for their future publishing roles as editors and publishers, especially for the possible application of new technologies to publishing.

Bibliographies

The problems of publishing specialised bibliographies in the humanities have been forcefully recounted in a personal communication by Margaret Child, Chief of the Research Services Division of the Smithsonian Institution Libraries. She writes:

> One problem which reaches across a number of humanistic disciplines ... concerns the need to find more stable sources of funding to support the 'publication' (in whatever format or by whatever means) of ongoing bibliographies. The current mission of the NEH's Research Resources Program ... does not cover the provision of ongoing support for a recurring activity such as the publication of an annual bibliography. Unfortunately, the learned societies which sponsor the compilation of such bibliographies are often small and do not have either the capital to underwrite a shift in production from a manual to an automated mode or sufficient

income to subsidise the annual issues. The situation is further complicated when the bibliography is a joint production of American and European scholars who often view the benefits of automation differently .... [One example] is the *International bibliography of Renaissance studies* where the problem of how to reduce the costs of production to a point low enough to have a reasonable expectation of being covered by annual subscriptions resulted in one American faction splitting off and starting a new computer-produced bibliography on its own .... [In some cases] bibliographies are still being compiled manually for lack of capital to cover the costs of conversion .... This not only means a more limited kind of bibliography in terms of indices, but also a long timelag between date of publication of the article and date of coverage by a published bibliography. I really do not see any way in which such publications can really become truly cost effective even if they are automated. That should reduce the expense of compiling, indexing and printing them but probably not enough in view of their limited market potential .... There is another twist to it as well in that the limited market makes such bibliographies unappealing to vendors of on-line databases .... And as reference work in libraries shifts increasingly to on-line searching, won't unavailability on-line put the humanist in the position of getting second-class service?

The Ad Hoc Committee on Basic Research Tools of the APA painted a similarly gloomy picture with regard to bibliographies dealing with the classics. It considered that increased user fees might provide an answer in the case of certain bibliographies, but pointed out that there were grave difficulties in this approach for international projects. The American offices of some international bibliographies were given hidden subsidies by their host institutions in the way of released time and the waiver of indirect costs, but the Committee concluded that:

> We do not think that most universities can be expected over the long run to pay all the costs of these projects, no matter what the gain to their prestige.

The only long-term solution, in the Committee's opinion, was for foundations to change their funding policies so that continuing projects of this kind could receive permanent regular support. It suggested that the ACLS was the logical equivalent of the European academies, and that the NEH and private foundations provide the funds in a block grant[22].

The problems encountered in publishing bibliographies are in many ways analogous to those of publishing small specialised humanities journals. The National Enquiry strongly recommended that where this was practicable, consortial arrangements might provide the advantages of economies of scale, so that the unit cost might be reduced. It also called on foundations to provide grants to encourage collaboration among publishers. The experience of the MLA illustrates how a large and experienced publisher can provide services to smaller bodies, on a cost-sharing basis. The MLA has long been committed to the idea of a 'humanities computer cooperative' and has made its facilities available to smaller societies at minimal cost. With the aid of substantial funding by the Mellon Foundation in 1979, it was able to increase the number of members of the MLA Consortium for Computer Services which now has 17 members spanning a wide range of humanities disciplines. The consortium provides them with a range of services including maintenance of membership files, accounting, the production of bibliographies and directories, and advice on other computer applications. The MLA aims to provide consortium members with photo-typesetting services in the near future.

Monographs

Another area of scholarly publishing where there are considerable problems is the publication of monographs. The specialised monograph is an extremely important vehicle for the dissemination of scholarly research in the humanities. In the USA, although learned societies and trade publishers publish scholarly books of this kind, it is the university presses which publish:

> most of the book-length scholarly work in the humanities .... University presses are subsidised presses. They were established because of the need to publish meritorious scholarly work that would not attract a large enough readership to warrant publication by commercial publishers[23].

Hence, the problems of publishing scholarly monographs tend to threaten the viability of American university presses.

Since the mid-1970s, these institutions have been faced by increased costs and declining unit sales of humanities monographs. Indeed, it was the sense of desperation evoked by the closure of a few university presses in those years that provided the spur for the establishment of the National Enquiry into Scholarly Communication in 1976, which concentrated its attention on the humanities. The Enquiry found that the sense of impending crisis was exaggerated but that the problems were:

> more persistent and difficult to handle ... not dramatic enough to kill the patient but able, if left unattended, to produce a lingering wasting disease[24].

The Enquiry's diagnosis still holds good. The patient has certainly not died, but survives in an economic climate that has become much harsher. Indeed, one university press director, Jack Goellner of the Johns Hopkins University Press (JHUP), believes that the fears of a crisis in the middle and later 1970s were merely a panic response by university presses to the first signs of recession and reduction of support by their parent institutions, but that the present time is one of genuine and increased difficulty for all university presses. There is a 'flatness' in the sales of scholarly monographs at present which is difficult to counteract. For example, at JHUP, in the first four months of production in 1982, although the costs of publication were no higher than had been predicted, sales were much lower. This seems to be the general experience among American university presses, and is mainly attributable to the reduced acquisition budgets of libraries, as well as to decreased activity in humanities departments in universities and colleges. Fewer students and faculty members mean fewer buyers for university press books, especially since there has been a general increase in the costs of production, editing and marketing. As a result, print runs are much lower; print runs for a scholarly monograph are now typically between 800 and 1,500 copies, whereas a few years ago they might have been nearer 2,500. At the same time, university press books are now kept in print for a much shorter time than before, with first printings often set for three years.

Title subsidies

In short, the situation delineated in the report of the National Enquiry regarding university presses and the publication of scholarly books remains essentially the same, although its effects have been intensified by inflation, recession and declining activity in humanities departments in higher education. The Enquiry stressed that market forces alone would never ensure that all meritorious works of scholarship in the humanities would be published, because the demand for some highly specialised works would always be limited. It therefore urged foundations to provide funds for title subsidies to support outstanding scholarly work which might otherwise be too expensive to publish. Since 1977, a small part of the budget of the NEH has been earmarked for title subsidies, mainly for the publication of research funded by the NEH, but also for other works which have not had prior support from the NEH. Indeed, in 1982, although the NEH was operating on a reduced budget overall, the publications programme was provided with increased funds[25]. But the most impressive programme of subsidies for the publication of scholarly books in the humanities has just been undertaken by the Mellon Foundation. It has allocated some $2,070,000 among 22 major university presses for the publication of humanities monographs. The money has been paid out in lump sums, so that the presses concerned can invest it, and benefit from the income, on condition that it is used over the next five years. A further $350,000 has been granted to the ACLS for allocation to some 10 or 12 smaller presses on a competitive basis.

3.4.4 Cooperative ventures in scholarly publishing

The Mellon Foundation has also awarded a grant of $50,000 to the Scholars Press, to launch a new series of inter-disciplinary monographs in the humanities. This press is a cooperative venture of about 10 learned societies mainly in the fields of religion and the classics, including, for example, the APA and the American Academy of Religion. All the selection and editorial work is done by scholars in the member societies, while the Scholars Press itself provides the production and distribution facilities. In providing financial support to this venture, the Mellon Foundation wished to encourage a cooperative organisation that provided an economically viable alternative to the publication of scholarly works by a university press.

In fact, the National Enquiry, as has been noted earlier, strongly maintained the need for cooperation and consortial arrangements between smaller university presses and larger established publishers in order to take advantage of economies of scale in production and distribution. Several cooperative ventures have been undertaken. For example, the JHUP runs a consortium with 20 university presses, and provides a range of services including order processing, data processing, warehousing and shipping and credit and cash management. One of the most recent attempts of this kind was a proposal in 1982 to set up a Center for Scholarly Publishing at the University of South Carolina, to make available information and to share a number of computer resources (ranging from consultation to sophisticated computer programs to prepare machine-readable files for typesetting) with university presses and other academic publishing organisations, thereby taking advantage of economies of scale to share the benefits of automated editing and production. The Center planned to cooperate with university presses, editors of scholarly editions and individual scholars, to share existing resources of hardware and software, and to develop other automated resources as needed. However, because so many university presses were fearful of how automation might change their own roles in publishing, the scheme was shelved.

One organisation that has attempted to encourage various forms of cooperative endeavour is the AAUP. It has been attempting to extend the market for American university press books overseas, and has sent exhibitions of university press books to Japan with this aim in mind and is planning an exhibition to China for 1984. It also sells mailing lists derived from its members, which include names and addresses of faculty members by subject, and of libraries, an activity which has proved to be profitable.

3.4.5 Other alternatives to increase the viability of scholarly publishing

While title subsidies can help to mitigate the acuteness of the problem of publishing particular specialist titles, they are a palliative, rather than a solution. Cooperative ventures are a far more fundamental expedient, but it has proved difficult in some cases to persuade publishers to combine operations in this way. Consequently, a number of other possibilities have been mooted. One is that university presses try to extend the range of their publishing operations, and try to break into the commercial and professional field. The danger of this approach is that university presses, in their attempts to become more like trade publishers in seeking more popular markets, might lose their *raison d'être* which is precisely to provide an outlet for specialist research that would otherwise not be published at all. In any event, there is a case for thinking that university presses often lack the financial and managerial resources of commercial publishers, particularly as far as marketing is concerned, and would therefore not be able to compete successfully with trade publishers.

Another possibility, which has been tried out by several university presses, is to become more specialised, by narrowing the range of their lists, concentrating on those fields in which they have established a reputation, rather than attempting to cover the whole range of disciplines. In this way, individual presses can establish their own special niche in the market, and concentrate their promotion and distribution activities. This approach, although a sensible one in itself, may be difficult to carry out in practice, particularly by state university presses, which are often expected to represent the whole spectrum of research in their publishing programme.

Author-prepared machine-readable output

Another expedient which is likely to increase in future is to pass on some of the costs of publishing to the author, especially the cost of composition, which often amounts, on average, to as much as 60% of the total cost of production of the finished book. As has already been noted, there has been an increased tendency for authors in the humanities to prepare their manuscripts on word processors, and this tendency will undoubtedly increase with time, as a new generation comes into being of authors and referees who own computers (or have easy access to them) and are familiar with their use. The use of word processors by authors could reduce upfront publishing costs by eliminating repetitive keyboarding, and reducing certain copy-editing and proof-reading costs. The great problem here is lack of standardisation, and the incompatibility between different brands of floppy disc and of word-processing equipment, and of computer typesetters.

As the Electronic Publishing Sub-Committee of the Association of American Publishers (AAP) pointed out recently:

The author's keystrokes are valuable only if the publisher's system can process them. The problem is, most publishing systems cannot economically or otherwise process input from all of the personal computers, word processors, electronic typewriters and mainframes that authors use for manuscript preparation. Each brand and class of hardware has its own unique set of internal codes, rendering it incompatible with devices of another brand or class.

The AAP is in the process of preparing 'a standard method for authors to keyboard their manuscripts ... that is device-independent ... compatible with publishing systems, and that is relatively easy and economical for authors to use' based on the ANSI/ISO standard for generic coding; this should result in the promulgation of American publishing industry standards and guidelines for authors and editors.

The two-year $250,000 project began in May 1983 and is administered by the AAP, the CLR and the National Bureau of Standards, with a review board of representatives of the LC, the Society for Scholarly Publishing, the AAUP, the National Federation of Abstracting and Indexing Services, the Authors' Guild and the STM (the international group of Scientific, Technical and Medical Publishers), as well as the publishers of major style manuals — the University of Chicago Press, the MLA, McGraw-Hill and ISI Press. The project will assess the extent to which publishers are attempting to capture and use author keystrokes, and will study the compatibility of various devices, formats, coding schemes, character sets and author/publisher conventions. A list of requirements for developing standard codes for formatting, and for bibliographic description, author and editor coding and keyboarding will then be prepared, in order to effect the standardisation of electronic text transmission in the USA. The project will enable authors to create a transferable electronic file that can be processed on any device and be used as input for any application. Publishers will be able to edit and proof-read that text on their machines and transmit formatted data for printing without any rekeyboarding. This project is also discussed in Section 5.2.2.

Two-tier publication

The use of computers to reduce some of the cost of publication will no doubt increase the viability of scholarly publishing. But many people feel that this does not go far enough. In view of the very limited demand for, and high cost of, producing and distributing certain types of specialist scholarly material, there is fairly considerable support in some publishing circles for the idea of a two-tier system of publication. Certain types of highly specialised manuscript would be published (after the normal refereeing process had first taken place) using a non-print format, say on microform, with hard copy available on demand, and with different marketing procedures. Only a proportion of the total output of publishing would be published in the traditional, conventional manner, with full editorial and promotional treatment. Such a solution would be extremely difficult to carry through, in view of the strong preference of authors (and of interviewing committees) for conventional modes of publication. At present, on-demand publications are likely to be thought of as inferior to fully published ones. A recent survey of deans of faculties[27] revealed that they would not regard candidates for faculty positions with online publications as being on a par with those with an equal number of conventional printed publications to their credit. The scholarly community is essentially conservative, and there is likely to be a considerable time-lag between the introduction of new methods of dissemination, which are perfectly feasible technologically, and their acceptance by those whom the communication system exists to serve.

3.5 Conclusion

Despite the effects of recession, there are a large number of initiatives taking place at present in the USA to improve the system of communication in the humanities. As a result of the increasing power and sophistication of computers, many of these initiatives are concerned with the application of computers to the solution of some of the most important problems of information transfer in the humanities. What still remains to be seen is how the introduction of new technologies into a very well-established system of communication will affect the way scholars work, and whether traditional communication patterns will be altered, or possibly even transformed. What is very evident as far as the humanities in the USA are concerned is that there is a growing conviction that all the institutions involved in the communication process, especially the scholars themselves, must consult together and take positive steps to see that technololgy is introduced for the benefit of scholarship, and not to its detriment.

3.6 References

1 *The humanities in American life.* Report of the Commission on the Humanities. Berkeley, Los Angeles, London, University of California Press, 1980. pp 1-3.

2 Ibid. p 27.

3 *Report of the Andrew W Mellon Foundation, 1981.* New York (1982). pp 10-14; Hooper, Judith. Fellowships in the humanities: protecting an endangered species. *Change,* October 1982, pp 43-44.

4 *Scholarly communication: the report of the National Enquiry.* Baltimore and London, JHUP, 1979. p xi.

5 USA. National Commission on Libraries and Information Science: Public Sector/Private Sector Task Force: *Public sector/private sector interaction in providing information services.* US Government Printing Office, 1982.

6 Alter, M. 'Proposal for the development of publishing industry standards and author guidelines on electronic manuscript preparation'. Association of American Publishers New Technology Committee, Electronic Publishing Sub-committee, 3 December 1982. *STM Innovation Bulletin* 5 in *STM Newsletter* 61, Amsterdam, January 1983; *The Chronicle of Higher Education,* 9 January 1983, p 27.

7 Haas, Warren J. 'Libraries and the humanities: technological aspects of knowledge handling.' Comments delivered at a conference at The Hague, 29 September-1 October 1982. (Paper kindly supplied by Mr Haas.)

8 Haas, Warren J. Computing in documentation and scholarly research. *Science,* Vol 215, no 4534, 12 February 1982, pp 857-861.

9 Ibid. p 858.

10 Marcum, Deanna B. 'Summary of the AAU/CLR Task Forces on Libraries.' Paper delivered at the annual meeting of the society for Scholarly Publishing, 1982.

11 *CLR Recent Developments,* 11 (1), January 1983, p 3.

12 *CLR Recent Developments,* 9 (2), August 1981; 10 (1-3), January-September 1982; 11(1), January 1983; CLR, *Twenty-fifth Annual Report,* 1981; RLG, *East Asian Studies,* August 1982.

13 Bearman, David. 'Towards national information systems: strategies and frameworks'. Paper read at a meeting of the Association of Canadian Archivists, 1 June 1982.

14 RLG, press release, 27 October 1982. 'NEH awards $143, 354 for RLG preservation project'.

15 CLR. *Twenty-fifth Annual Report,* pp 30-31; *CLR Recent Developments,* 10 (3), September 1982, p 3.

16 Cyert, Richard M and Knapp, Peggy A. 'Research in the humanities'. 10 September 1982. (Unpublished paper kindly made available by Dr David Breneman, Brookings Institution, Inc.)

17 A conversation with William J Bennett. *Humanities,* 3 (2), April 1982, p 4.

18 Farr, George. Research tools and reference works — part III. *Humanities,* 3 (1), February 1982.

19 Ibid.

20 Rütimann, Hans. 'The role of the scholarly society' 1982? Mackesy, Eileen M. 'The MLA Thesaurus of Linguistic, Literary and Folkloric Terms: a work in progress'. (Unpublished papers kindly made available by Dr Rütimann.)

21 *Scholarly communication,* op cit, p 10.

22 Bagnall, Roger S. *Research tools for the classics.* Chico, California, Scholars Press, 1980.

23 *Scholarly communication,* op cit, pp 80-81.

24 Ibid. p 3.

25 *Humanities,* 3 (1), February 1982, p 22.

26 Alter, op cit, pp 4-5.

27 Seiler, Lauren H and Raben, Joseph. The electronic journal. *Society,* 18 (6) September/October 1981, pp 76-83.

4 The Office for Humanities Communication, by Dr M Katzen

The Office for Humanities Communication was established at the University of Leicester in November 1982 by the BLR&D Department to act as a focus for research and dissemination of information in this field. It was originally set up as an experimental venture, for 18 months, but following a discussion at the first meeting of its Advisory Panel, it was felt that its objectives would be carried out more effectively by extending its initial period of operation to last until June 1986. The Office is under the direction of Professor AJ Meadows, the Project Head, and its activities are carried out by Dr M Katzen, the Project Manager, and a part-time secretary. Overall guidance is provided by its Advisory Panel which meets twice a year. This consists of three academic advisors (one of whom represents the British Academy, with which the Office maintains close touch) and two representatives of the British Library.

The Office for Humanities Communication is the first attempt to establish a continuing integrated programme of systematic work related to problems of communication in the humanities in the UK, and follows a number of initiatives, including several conferences and a number of research projects funded by the BLR&D Department in this field for almost a decade. In fact, the Office is almost certainly the only one of its kind anywhere in the world so far. In 1979, as described in Section 3.1, the National Enquiry into Scholarly Communication (which focused on communication problems in the humanities in the USA) strongly recommended that a similar, but more narrowly conceived, project, the Office for Scholarly Communication, be set up within the NEH, but nothing came of this. In May 1982, as Chapter 2 reports, an Anglo-American conference of scholars and members of funding agencies on both sides of the Atlantic met in the UK to discuss problems of information and communication in both countries, and recommended that such offices be set up both in the USA and in the UK. In the UK, the BLR&D Department acted on this recommendation and set up the Office for Humanities Communication six months later. In the USA, the ACLS commissioned a report by Dr Herbert C Morton on this matter early in 1983 (see Chapter 5) and is now taking steps to set up a parallel office in the USA, the Office of Scholarly Communication and Technology; there seems every likelihood that it will be established in the near future. In that case, there will be a firm institutional basis for liaison, and for joint research and educational ventures related to information and communication in the UK and the USA. The UK Office also plans to establish and maintain close contacts with scholars, funding agencies and learned societies in European countries. Plans are afoot to hold a series of binational meetings similar in scope to the Anglo-American meeting, which will lay the basis for close liaison with relevant institutions in Europe.

The Office for Humanities Communication has three main objectives:

1. To provide an active focus for the systematic study of the communication of information in the humanities in the UK, by identifying current modes of communication, and any barriers and dislocations which might impede the efficient flow of information in this field, and by suggesting directions in which future research might usefully be applied.

2. To promote an awareness of the importance of communication activities, especially those related to the application of new technologies, among scholars in humanities disciplines in the UK, by disseminating information about these matters in various ways (e.g. meetings, demonstrations, newsletters).

3. To maintain contact with relevant bodies, including learned societies and funding agencies, in other countries, especially in North America and Western Europe, and, where this seems desirable and feasible, to engage in joint research and educational activities.

A brief account of some of the activities already undertaken or under way at present will provide concrete examples of the range and scope of the Office's work.

The first venture to be undertaken under the aegis of the Office was a three-week study tour of the East coast of the USA in October-November 1982, to identify recent initiatives relating to the communication of information in the humanities there (see Chapter 3). This was a valuable exercise, both for information gathering and for liaison.

A comprehensive questionnaire survey has been carried out, directed to members of staff of humanities departments, libraries and computer service departments in all universities and polytechnics in the UK. The survey aimed to elicit information on a range of topics related to communication in the humanities, including the amount and type of instruction provided for undergraduates and postgraduates in locating pertinent reference material, in preparing material for publication, and in the use of computers for information retrieval, research, and dissemination of research results, as well as information on the use of new technologies in research and manuscript preparation by members of staff. The mail survey will be followed up by a number of intensive, semi-structured interviews. The intention of the survey is to gain a comprehensive picture of current activities in these fields as a basis for planning future research, and to make contact with key individuals around whom this research might be planned.

A series of one-day demonstrations, on the applications of computers to research in the humanities, is in the course of being held for academics in humanities departments in various parts of the country. The demonstrations cover information retrieval, text manipulation and text processing, and include formal presentations by experts, 'hands on' experience for participants, and case studies. The first demonstration was held at Oxford in the Oxford University Computing Centre in February 1983; the second and third took place in London in May and September 1983 respectively. The first demonstration was intended for senior academics in universities within a reasonable range of Oxford. The second and third were focused on members of staff in universities and polytechnics in and around London who were interested in but not very knowledgeable about the field. The aim of these demonstrations is to promote an awareness among scholars of the potentialities of computers in such areas as online retrieval, database construction, text manipulation and word processing. The first three demonstrations were concerned to show computer applications in a variety of fields in the humanities. They will be followed by a series of meetings aimed at academics doing research in particular disciplines, including music and history, which will focus on the special applications of computers in these fields.

Another project which is under way at present is specifically geared to the use of computerised databases. An experimental bibliographic database is being mounted on a TransAm Tuscan microcomputer, and it will be demonstrated to students and members of staff in humanities departments round the country. The aims of the demonstration are to illustrate the usefulness of online database searching, using the microcomputer as a surrogate for mainframe database searching, as well as to indicate how personal computers can be used to compile personalised bibliographic databases. The first experimental database consists of bibliographic records relating to 18th century English literature. The second database consists of records derived from a variety of sources, relating to British and Irish political, economic and social history of the 18th century. It is possible that others may be added, following the results of a few experimental demonstrations.

The whole topic of databases on microcomputers is one which appears to have interesting potential for future research, particularly in relation to the question of downloading records from online databases to local computer stores, and the implications for publishers, libraries and users.

The Office has also begun to issue a newsletter, the *Humanities Communication Newsletter,* which will provide an alerting service, mainly for academics, librarians and computer service departments in institutions of higher learning in the UK, on current developments in communication in the humanities in the UK and elsewhere. It is hoped that it will also be of interest to learned societies and publishers. The newsletter will appear irregularly, about twice a year.

In 1984, a series of interviews and discussion groups will be undertaken with members of staff of universities, learned societies and publishers to identify current difficulties in information and communication related to the humanities, and the actual and potential use of new technologies, as well as to promote awareness of the importance of communication. These activities will act as an aid in identifying the direction in which further research and dissemination might most usefully be applied.

5 Scholarly communication and technology: a proposal, by Dr Herbert C Morton

The following paper has kindly been made available for inclusion in this report by the ACLS. The ACLS commissioned the report from Dr Herbert Morton early in 1983. It was approved by the Board of Directors of the ACLS in October 1983, and the President of the ACLS was authorised to seek the necessary funding to establish the Office of Scholarly Communication and Technology. The paper, originally prepared for internal use, is reproduced here as presented to the ACLS, with only minor corrections and deletions. The paper is also to appear in a forthcoming issue of the journal *Scholarly Publishing*.

5.1 Introduction

A film was made the night the *New York Times* was produced for the last time by the traditional hot-metal technology. The camera lingered over scenes of linotype operators setting type, printers making up pages and locking them into steel chases, the stereotyping of pages for the rotary presses. That was 1978, and by then the new electronic technology was well-established in the newspaper business. In book and journal publishing, however, the changeover was taking place more slowly. The linotype and letterpress printing had been largely superseded during the 1970s by photocomposition and offset reproduction (though both technologies still survive where certain aesthetic qualities are highly desired), but for a number of reasons the second phase of the transition — the introduction of the new computer-assisted technology — was more talked about than used. Writers, editors and printers continued to work at their separate tasks much as they had in the past. The second step — perfecting the machine-readable system whereby words move in machine-readable form from word processor to typesetter to electronic pagination to camera and to the press — is the task for the 1980s. The system works, but it is being exploited fully for only a small proportion of books and journals.

In libraries the transformation is moving along the same dramatic lines. Manual cataloguing of library collections is being replaced by online cataloguing. The scholar's domain, which was mostly limited to nearby collections, has been extended greatly by bibliographic networks that promise to bring almost the totality of the nation's resources within reach. New technologies are being employed in storage and in preservation. But for libraries, as well as for printers and publishers, the changeover has not been without frustration and heavy cost; difficult times lie ahead for them and their constituencies.

The scholarly community that has been trying to adjust to the consequences of the new technology has, at the same time, been shaken by other powerful forces that raised costs and cut revenues. Graduate enrolments, particularly in the humanities, suffered declines. Rapidly rising prices drove up the costs of university operations and eroded the purchasing power of endowment incomes. A slowdown in economic activity reduced federal revenues and led to cutbacks in numerous government programmes. Academic libraries were driven to adopt cost-cutting measures, as were learned societies and scholarly publishers. Scholarly book and journal publishing has also been affected. This litany of hard times is a familiar one, and when viewed in the light of the technological revolution it encouraged the search for appropriate responses.

Among the responses considered within the system of scholarly communications has been the establishment of an office of scholarly communication to monitor the nature of the changes under way, their effects, and the results. Recommendation 11 of the report of the National Enquiry into Scholarly Communication suggested that an Office of Scholarly Communication be set up in the NEH. There was support for the proposal within NEH, which had contributed to the financing of the National Enquiry, and a follow-up study on the proposal was conducted. The timing was not right, however, either financially or politically, and no action was taken.

Meanwhile the ACLS Committee on Scholarly Communication, which was set up in response to the Enquiry's emphasis on the need to sustain interest in the field and in particular to monitor new technology, concluded that it would be more appropriate to set up the Office within the private sector under ACLS auspices. The ACLS responded by commissioning this report.

5.1.1 British and Canadian experience

The concerns that were being felt in the USA echoed those felt in the UK and Canada, where public support of scholarly communication has been substantial.

In the UK an Office for Humanities Communication was established in November 1982 as an outgrowth of a conference of British and American representatives held the preceding spring under the auspices of the Primary Communications Research Centre of Leicester

University and the ACLS (see Chapter 2).

The Centre had been established by the BLR&D Department in the mid-1970s to conduct research on communications, to foster better liaison among participants in the communications process, and to disseminate information through publications and conferences. 'Primary' in the title refers to primary communication of research results, and the purview of the Centre is roughly comparable to scholarly communication as discussed in this report.

The Office for Humanities Communication, which evolved from the spring 1982 conference, gave greater visibility to the particular problems of the humanities, which had been the focus of concern in the USA. Initially funded for a period of 18 months, it was staffed by one professional (a member of the Centre staff), and a part-time secretary.

Two activities were promptly undertaken in early 1983 by the new Office. One is a survey of British universities and polytechnics to see what training in communication techniques is currently given to students in the humanities, both at undergraduate and postgraduate levels, and what use is being made of computers. In addition, one-day demonstrations to show how computers can simplify the mechanics of research and promote new research (such as textual analysis) were mounted at Oxford and in London. The demonstrations stressed retrieval of information, use of word processors, and manipulation of text by computer to produce indexes, bibliographies, and so on.

The Canadian government has long provided direct support to publishers of scholarly books and journals through the Social Science and Humanities Research Council of Canada. Between 1970 and 1978, the number of applications for grants increased five-fold, as did the amount of money provided. Then the number of applications levelled off. In 1981 grants totalling $1,270,000 were given to 95 journals out of 123 that applied. Even so, a growing number of editors reported difficulty in keeping up with rising costs. Many of them said they had to cut back on the number of pages printed, seek out cheaper printers, and do more work in-house.

Government support for scholarly books, which dates back to the 1940s, has also grown, from a handful of grants annually to about 150 by 1981. The programme was budgeted for $1,000,000 in 1981-82. Print runs for these subsidised books averaged 1,500 copies (though they varied considerably from book to book) and the subsidy provided about half the production cost. Procedures for making the awards are similar to those guiding the journals programme; an outside group makes the selection on merit.

These two programmes have contributed greatly to scholarly publication in Canada, but by the late 1970s there was little prospect that the grants programme would be able to keep up with rising needs; nor was there evidence that further cost-cutting efficiencies could help much in reducing rising deficits, though the book programme has a high administrative cost, largely owing to readers' fees and efforts to help authors find publishers. As a result, a reassessment was called for in 1979, and two years later a sub-committee submitted a report to the Social Science and Humanities Research Council of Canada. The report urged the exploration of new technologies and other means to meet the needs of scholarly communication and the goals of the Council expressed in its 1981 report: wider and more rapid dissemination of research results and greater accessibility of these materials to users.

The references to technology strike a cautious note. 'It is not appropriate to adopt, in advance, a dogmatic position regarding the relative benefits of traditional and newer modes .... The potential of these technologies ... is sufficiently great that it merits exploration and development with assistance from public funds.' The report added, however, that the Council has an obligation to stimulate cost-effective improvement in the use of the traditional modes.

The report met a mixed response and has generated considerable discussion. Modifications of the recommendations were still under discussion in the spring of 1983.

One gets the impression that both in Canada and the UK the government plays a strong direct role in efforts to strengthen scholarly communication. Partnership with the private sector is less apparent, private foundations playing a larger role in the USA. Lessons from the British experience are likely to be more applicable to an American Office.

5.1.2   The limits of a piecemeal approach

Periodically, over a couple of decades, the scholarly community has become alarmed by conditions in scholarly publishing, in research libraries, and in related aspects of research and dissemination. Finances have been one major concern, but surely not the only one. Questions of comparable importance have been raised about how the system is functioning — whether it is fulfilling the needs of researchers who have results to publish and of users who want easy access to what has been published. The rapid pace of technological change and its impact keep raising new questions, and the response to a new question, or to a gnawing concern, is to commission a new study.

Clearly, on the basis of these repeated efforts, the underlying issues must be judged to be important and persistent. However, the historical piecemeal process of dealing with them seems quite unsuitable for coping with perennial issues with long-run implications. Information gets to be out of date. Emerging problems are not identified until they become major issues. Research on the problems is not additive. There is no sense of continuity, and each study faces costly start-up expenses and delays. The evidence of recent years — both in what has been published about scholarly communication and in what needs to be done — clearly points to the need for sustained effort. It seems time to establish an Office of Scholarly Communication and Technology to focus on the questions and carry out the functions described in this report.

5.2 The new technologies

At the heart of the revolution in information sciences, including the system of scholarly communication, is the computer which has made it possible to produce old products in remarkable new ways, to produce entirely new products, and to think about problems from a fresh perspective.

In the world of publishing, the computer has left some products unchanged while transforming the way in which they are made. The book today is virtually indistinguishable from the book a century ago, but it is the product of an entirely new industry. Some aspects of the making of it — such as the electronic photocomposition machines — accomplish in seconds what the old hot metal technology required hours to do. Along with speed has come greater flexibility and, when the technology is efficiently employed, lower cost. At the same time, the computer has opened up the possibility of new modes to supplement the book, such as electronic publishing that bypasses print and book shelves. In contrast to the trend toward mass production of thousands, and even millions, of copies of the same manuscript, the computer makes possible the retrieval and scrutiny of information tailored to the needs of an individual, and it can do so in a matter of seconds.

Similarly the library building on campus or in the local community looks much the same, with its book stacks and reading rooms, but computer terminals are becoming more visible, offering new ways to search the libraries' own holdings as well as other information sources. Storage of archival materials in the original, printed form is being supplemented not only by the microform technology but by magnetic tapes and optical discs which achieve enormous savings in space and in time. The borrowing of books goes on largely as it always has, except that the system for recording transactions has been greatly speeded up and improved by the introduction of computer systems in many libraries.

In the schools, much of the routine of teachers and pupils remains unchanged, but in some classes where drill is important, such as mathematics and languages, computer-assisted programmes have proved to be very effective supplements. With the rapid spread of computers that has been predicted, the development of new software could introduce a much richer educational experience than the routines now available.

The enormous impact of the computer is a reflection not only of its capacities but also of its rapid deployment. This familiar story has been summed up in a vivid if somewhat oversimplified fashion by a leading management consultant as follows:

in the 1950s, a large company could afford a computer;

in the 1960s, a company division could afford one;

in the 1970s, a department could afford one;

in the 1980s, an individual could afford a computer;

in the 1990s, nearly everyone will have a computer.

In some 30 years, the computer thus has moved from the laboratory into the home, changing along the way from a major piece of capital equipment to an ordinary consumer product. The market is being developed and expanded for a wide range of computer products and related technologies such as the video disc, and the pace of innovation continues to be rapid.

Both the speed and the revolutionary nature of the changes under way in computers and related techniques are so great that the non-specialist can keep up with only the general outlines and with those applications that affect him or her directly. But the specialists must go farther. In the field of scholarly communication, publishers are working hard not only to keep up with what the new technology has to offer but to help direct it. The AAP is promoting the acceptance of a generic coding that would greatly facilitate the transfer of information from word processors to photocomposition machines. Similarly, librarians are trying to apply new technology to problems of information storage and dissemination, mindful both of the technological possibilities and of the needs of users for whom change may be relatively attractive or intrusive, and cognisant of differences, for example, between how scientists seek and use information and how humanists do.

The new products and services include the innovative equipment — mainframe computers, minicomputers, microcomputers, word processors, and so on — which produces the old products, and the entirely new services, such as database networks and online information services, that create new products. The computer gives promise of being one of those pervasive technologies, like the automobile, which creates a large supporting system of industries and alters living styles. With the auto came the nationwide system of highways, the rise of the petroleum industry, the chains of retail gas stations, garage repair businesses, motels and roadside restaurants, and the exodus to the suburbs. While the computer is hardly likely to give rise to so many supporting industries, the potential pervasiveness of its impact on factory production, employment, retail operations of all types, the knowledge industry in all its aspects, and on home life is difficult to calculate fully. (Not all the effects are disruptive. A prominent publisher, taunted about the inroads of the computer on reading and book sales, quipped that he was not worried so long as he continued to sell about nine books for every computer that reached the market.)

The computer has also altered the way problems are conceptualised. With regard to gathering and disseminating information, a researcher may think not simply about writing a book, but rather about establishing a database, which in turn can be adapted to many different uses — printing a publication in parts or in its entirety, electronic distribution, or storage and retrieval on demand.

The central question facing the groups that collectively constitute the system of scholarly communication is how to keep informed about what is happening. The corollary issue is how to influence both the pace and direction of change in ways that will enhance the acquisition and use of knowledge. Leaders in the library, publishing, and scholarly constituencies recognise the need to enlarge their concerns beyond the needs of their special group, be it libraries or publishing, to the welfare of the total system. This was a major theme of the report of the National Enquiry into Scholarly Communication in 1979. And it is a central concern of the ACLS today as it considers the establishment of an Office of Scholarly Communication and Technology. How could such an Office contribute to the ability of the sytem of scholarly communication to adjust to, and influence the application of, new technology?

Figure 5.1. Computerisation of bibliographic processes: highlights since 1961

Date	Events
1961	Development of Medical Literature Analysis and Retrieval System (MEDLARS), the basis for the first automated library bibliographic network. In batch mode, the system permitted rapid printing of *Index Medicus,* the bibliography of current medical literature.
1961	Institute for Scientific Information and *Science Citation Index* established. This and subsequently developed indexes for other areas use citation frequency to organize literature and to map research progression in specific fields.
1965	Information Transfer Experiment (INTREX) conducted at MIT to store, retrieve, and transmit scientific information electronically.
1965	Conference of Library of Congress staff and academic librarians to explore bibliographic automation. One result was development of Machine-Readable Cataloging (MARC), now the standard communications format for bibliographic information.
1967	Ohio College Library Center created. OCLC evolved to become the largest bibliographic service system, supporting shared cataloging, interlibrary loan, and acquisitions.
1968 to 1974	Rapid growth of commercial on-line search services, including DIALOG, ORBIT, and Bibliographic Retrieval Service (BRS).
1970	University of Chicago Library development of comprehensive Library Data Management System to computerize and integrate primary library functions.
1972	MEDLARS converted from batch to on-line system, MEDLINE.
1972	Bibliographic utility formed at University of Toronto. Shared cataloging and other services were gradually developed and extended to Canadian libraries and, in 1980, to the United States.
1973	Conversion of Serials (CONSER) project begun, the first full-scale effort to build a machine-readable database of records contributed by a group of cooperating libraries.

64

1973   Research Libraries Group formed. The organization now operates the Research Libraries Information Network bibliographic service and supports cooperative programs in collection development and preservation.

1973   Universal Bibliographic Control (UBC) established. This continuing program of the International Federation of Library Associations and Institutions promotes development of national bibliographies and international exchange of standardized bibliographic records.

1974   BALLOTS, an on-line technical processing service, developed by the Stanford University Libraries.

1976   Washington Library Network (WLN) established. The Washington state legislature supported development of the first authority-controlled bibliographic network, now used by libraries of all types in the Pacific Northwest.

1978   Bibliographic Service Development Program established by the Council on Library Resources. With the goal of establishing a nationwide bibliographic service, the program promotes cooperation among bibliographic services of all kinds among academic and research libraries. It funds and manages projects, including on-line catalog development, creation of name authority file service, and functional linking of existing computerized services.

1981   Library of Congress "freezes" its card catalog. Records for items added to Library of Congress collections after 1 January 1981 are added only to computerized bibliographic systems.

Source: Warren J Haas. Computing in documentation and scholarly research. *Science,* 12 February 1982, p 860.

5.2.1   Libraries and bibliographic services

The information explosion and a series of innovations in electronic technology began to put new pressures on libraries more than two decades ago. Since then, demands for service and new tools for coping with them have moved almost hand-in-hand, and there has been a change in the concept of what a library is and does. Increasingly, it has become a channel of access to information, with greater attention to resource sharing. Even the biggest and richest libraries can no longer be virtually self-sufficient.

The 1960s saw great advances in the storage and retrieval of information and development of huge computerised databases which dwarfed old manual bibliographies and provided faster service. Online services followed, which not only enabled the individual to find information almost instantaneously but also permitted interaction with the computer and the modification of the search in new directions in response to the information being received. Although the vision of a new, single, national bibliographic system faded more than a decade ago when the full dimensions of the task were realised, a *de facto* system has been taking shape through the linking of well-established components. These include the LC, the RLG, the WLN, and the National Library of Medicine which developed MEDLARS, the Medical Literature Analysis and Retrieval System, considered to be the first automated library bibliographic network, in 1961 and which went online a decade later as MEDLINE. (See Figure 5.1 for a list of major bibliographic developments.)

During the late 1960s and early 1970s, commercial online database services began to operate. Initially, they dealt primarily with medical, business, and scientific data, but gradually they added social science and humanistic bibliographies. Today, one of the largest humanistic databases, the *International bibliography* of the MLA, is available from two of the major services, DIALOG and BRS.

From bibliographic retrieval, the search services moved to the provision of full text. In journalism, for example, full text was provided for the *New York Times*. In June 1983 the American Chemical Society put the full text of its journals online.

'Full text', at the moment, is something of a misnomer because the searcher gets something less than what is carried in the original. Only the words are transmitted. Charts, graphs, and formulae are not included. Only when the optical video disc is introduced will a truly full-text service be available.

The pace of development is dazzling, and one is hard pressed to keep up. In spring 1983, for example, the librarian who was content with the *New York Times* online service would have learned that the service was being taken over by NEXIS, a service of Mead Data Central, which pioneered in 1973 with an online service for lawyers, called LEXIS. NEXIS is a prodigious resource for those interested in current affairs. It offers the full text of some 80 newspapers, magazines, and wire services, going back to 1975 for some magazines and to 1977 for some newspapers. The service is next day for papers and 12-24 hours after release for wire services. It clearly is an enhanced service, but for the librarian faced with both expanding requests for information and fixed amounts of money and space, the shift of the *New York*

Times to NEXIS presents a problem. NEXIS is available only on a dedicated terminal and can be obtained only by subscription — two requirements that did not exist under the old *New York Times* service. Ohio College Library Center (OCLC) already requires libraries to have a dedicated terminal. How many more can be kept by a modest-sized library? Additional space is required, and monthly subscription fees are added to online costs.

Full text does offer one clear advantage for searching: it reduces a researcher's dependence on the judgments of indexers and abstracters but gets access to the exact words used by the author. On the other hand, it does require a familiarity with the source vocabulary.

NEXIS, DIALOG, and BRS are part of a much larger and fast-growing community of database systems developed for information access and retrieval. In 1982, *Science* reported that there were about 1,000 different information retrieval systems, up from 400 a year earlier. And these in turn draw on the universe of more than 15,000 databases.

DIALOG, for example, advertised in 1983 access to 60 million references from over 150 databases covering science, technology, business, medicine, social science, current affairs, and the humanities. It claims that the average search costs $5 to $15 and requires no subscription fee. BRS claims 40 million references from a substantially smaller list of databases, but the subject scope is similar to DIALOG's. Unlike DIALOG, BRS requires a subscription fee. Like DIALOG, it is continually acquiring new databases.

The MLA bibliography has been available through DIALOG for over five years and more recently from BRS as well. (It had been computerised even earlier and maintained by a service bureau, so data are now available back to 1970.) The experience of a database owner provides perspective.

Over the decade the biggest change in the MLA bibliography was the preparation of a subject file, financed by a grant from the NEH. Users had complained that the finding system no longer permitted scholars to find what they wanted. New fields of interest and new emphases made traditional author and title files inadequate. If one wanted to search the file for references to women in literature or women's issues, for example, there was no way to do so. (The importance of subject searches was recently confirmed again by the online catalogue survey reported below.) The MLA's subject file was introduced with the edition for 1981.

The building of a constituency for online use of the bibliography has developed very gradually, and for a time it was uncertain whether DIALOG would want to continue the file. Use of the file remains modest compared to the use of scientific databases, but it has increased nearly four-fold since the early years when it averaged about 20 hours a month.

Income is commensurately modest, accounting for only about 2% of the MLA's royalty income. Printed materials still constitute the biggest source of MLA income. (As for the online database industry generally, one estimate is that 20-40% of royalty income is obtained from online sources. It will be many years — if ever — before income from the database begins to rival income from the printed sources.)

Ironically, perhaps, the work on the computerised database itself contributed to the usefulness of the printed volume, first by speeding up the entire bibliographical and printing process and secondly by making possible spin-off volumes from the complete bibliography. Thus, while most research libraries want the complete package, other libraries may now get along with less, and for individual scholars, purchase of a portion of the work for ready reference is a modest expenditure.

The financial success of the bibliographical system and related activities is reflected in the fact that the MLA now depends on dues to cover less than 20% of its budget, compared with the typical 50-70% for learned societies. This achievement has been possible, in part, because of the adoption of a realistic pricing policy that requires users to pay for the services they get. To obtain the greatly improved and more timely bibliography, library users now have to pay more than double what they used to pay, but they can still get a less complete package for about what they used to pay. By and large, libraries have preferred to buy the complete package; the better bibliography is worth the added cost. Though it is priced high in comparison to standard books and directories in the humanities, the bibliography is not expensive when compared to reference works in the sciences.

A number of lessons emerge from the MLA experience. The obvious one is that if the humanities are to take advantage of the possibilities of the new technology, as have the sciences and, to a lesser extent, some of the social sciences, they will have to recognise that a better product costs more money. Thus, if the project is to survive, it must be priced at a level that will fully cover the costs, at least, and eventually contribute to overhead costs and to a working fund that will finance further research and development projects. If the price is too high in relation to the benefits of the service, the project will not survive. Doubtless some bibliographic projects will prove not to be self-supporting — in which case the scholarly community will have to decide whether limited funds for subsidy should support such a project in the face of competition from alternative uses of the money.

Secondly, conversion to a new system is expensive and needs subsidisation. Launching the MLA effort required substantial grants from the Mellon Foundation and the NEH. The development costs were far beyond the resources of a learned society and the uncertainty was too great for MLA to go it alone. But after the initial grants were made, the project became self-sustaining. The foundation commitment was essential, it was temporary, and it paid off. The experience was instructive and encouraging to both MLA and its supporters.

Thirdly, a large innovative project imposes difficult choices, days of uncertainty, and nights of worry, and, to succeed, it demands considerable entrepreneurial and managerial skills.

A leader in the effort to link bibliographic systems has been the CLR, founded by the Ford Foundation in 1956. The CLR has worked with other groups to promote cooperation within the library and bibliographic world and to encourage new research by awarding millions of dollars for special studies, including one recently completed on online cataloguing. Since libraries are responsible for providing services to users, they must not only find out what is feasible, efficient, and economical, they also must be responsive to what users want. Thus, though there has long been no question about the technical feasibility of switching from manual card catalogues to online catalogues of a library's holdings, there has been some uncertainty about whether users — not only in research libraries, but in public libraries as well — would resist or resent the change or find difficulty in using it. Consequently, the CLR sponsored a national survey of user response to online cataloguing to find out how the system might be improved and made easier for patrons to use. The survey sampled the views of 8,000 library patrons who had used the online catalogue and 4,000 patrons who had not. Twenty-nine libraries, representing 15 different online catalogue systems, participated in the survey, under the aegis of five participating organisations.

The 152-page final report of the results showed that nine out of 10 persons who used the online catalogue liked it. Three out of four said they preferred the online catalogue to the system it replaced. Support for the online system increased with frequency of use. Similarly, those who had not used the online catalogue thought that they could learn to use it quickly and easily and were willing to try. Their reason for not having used the catalogue was usually the lack of time to learn about it rather than dislike or fear of computers.

A profile of users, suggested by the survey results, indicates that users are predominantly male and relatively young. They are usually undergraduates interested in the humanities and engaged in searching for materials for class use. The major purpose of the research is to obtain material for preparation of papers.

The survey also yielded helpful information about how catalogues are used. Subject files clearly are the most important (MLA studies had pointed to the same conclusion). Also highly valued is the ability to search tables of contents and indexes of books, to get information on circulation status and availability of holdings, and to be able to print the results.

Other projects supported by the CLR in cooperation with the library community include a study being carried out at the University of Michigan to assess the effectiveness of a system that combines remote storage of less-used books with an online search system, with assured 24-hour delivery of wanted items; the preparation of a computerised inventory of research collections, in which holdings will be classified in five grades, from trivial to exhaustive; and the BSDP, a five-year programme which in 1982 embraced 40 projects, supported by grants totalling $2 million. Among them is the Linked Systems project, which is intended to develop, coordinate, and link the bibliographic and computer system of the WLN, the RLG and the LC. The CLR has also set up a Task Force on Library Issues, composed of university presidents, librarians, and scholars.

Bibliographic access is only one of many technological issues of concern to librarians. Document delivery has become an increasing concern as access has improved. The possibilities of electronic publishing raise new questions. And, overall, advancing technology is imposing new financial burdens that will require creative solutions. These matters are under continuing discussion within individual libraries, at library meetings such as the recent annual meetings of the ARL, and in library publications.

Preservation also continues to rank high on the agenda of library concerns. Deterioration of even relatively recent books and journals has been extensive, owing to the use of acidic papers during the past century and a half. Three somewhat different requirements are apparent today. One is the technological need to devise better techniques for de-acidifying paper in order to arrest deterioration. Recent research at the LC and elsewhere has demonstrated the feasibility of new technology that permits de-acidification of even fragile books with considerable speed and efficiency, and further improvement can be expected. A second is the greater use of acid-free papers. Publishers are being urged to use acid-free papers in printing scholarly books and other works that are expected to have a long shelf life. A third is the management of a systematic approach to preservation that will ensure the maintenance of essential collections with a minimum of duplicated effort. There is a consensus on the need for preservation, work is proceeding, and further research and testing is being encouraged. What is at issue is the amount of money to be spent for this effort, and the source of funds.

5.2.2 Printing and publishing

The potential savings in time and money inherent in electronic publishing were grasped and applied first in journalism. Daily newspapers and weeklies such as the *Chronicle of Higher Education* and *US News and World Report* were in command of the new technology when book and journal publishers were still thinking about its possibilities. Reporters wrote their stories at computer terminals and revised them on cathode-ray screens, editors checked the articles on the screens before clearing them for photo-typesetting. In effect, writers had also become typesetters because of the capacity of photocomposition machines to read the output from the computer terminals.

What slowed the application of this machine-readable technology to books and journals was the publishers' lack of control over the original keyboarding. Whereas writing, keyboarding, typesetting, make-up, and printing was an integrated operation at newspapers and magazines, it was a fragmented operation in conventional book and journal publishing. Authors who used word processors or mainframe computers were working with scores of different hardware and software systems. These systems were not compatible with the photocomposition systems installed by printers — although some printing salesmen were rather cavalier in assuring authors and publishers that the problems of compatibility could readily be solved. Thus, when the report of the National Enquiry was being written in 1979, it was put on a word processor in the belief that after the final draft was approved, a disc could be given to a printer for virtually overnight photocomposition. But the printer's equipment could not read the electronic output submitted by the authors, and the entire report had to be rekeyboarded. There were, of course, occasional successes in the late 1970s in achieving machine readability, but many of these achievements were costly. The industry learned by doing — sometimes at the expense of the customer.

Since the late 1970s, the so-called 'black box' devices such as the Shaffstall have made it possible for publishers to work out operating patterns that have greatly increased the use of machine-readable discs and tapes prepared by authors. Scholarly publishers can cite examples where they have succeeded in using the technology, though most publishing still depends primarily on typed manuscripts. The feasibility of the machine-readable technology for book publishing today seems to be about where the enthusiasts claimed it was four or five years ago. It is clearly workable if sufficient advance planning takes place in many, if not all, situations, but it is not always economical where it is technically feasible. A typesetting house will tell a publisher what word-processing systems it prefers to handle and the range of systems that it can accept with more or less difficulty. Similarly, the publisher can choose between having typesetter output printed out in camera-ready galleys that can be made up into pages by hand, or having the pages made up electronically according to instructions about margins, headings, footnotes, page depth,and so on, that have been pre-programmed by commercial systems such as PENTA PAGE. PENTA now also offers the flexibility of light pens that make possible additional adjustment with a stroke of the pen.

Princeton University, one of the few university presses that operate their own printing plant, has prepared a memorandum to authors, explaining the equipment it has and the kinds of word-processor output it can accept, and what other steps an author can take to simplify the handling of machine-readable output. In this way it hopes to encourage greater use of the system.

In the long run, however, the success of machine-readable systems will depend on standardisation of equipment and software rather than on increasing cleverness in making incompatible machines compatible. Thus, the AAP is working out a plan to achieve compatibility over the next few years. In this effort it has enlisted the support of a group of more than 20 'stakeholders' in the enterprise, including the National Bureau of Standards, the Printing Industry Association, the Authors League of America, the Council of Engineering and Scientific Society Executives, the LC, the National Library of Medicine, the RLG, the ACLS and the authors and publishers of the principal style manuals. The list is heavily weighted with users, but the AAP is optimistic that its project eventually will win the support of the word processor and computer manufacturers. It awarded a $250,000 contract in July 1983 for the completion of a series of tasks leading, over the next two years, to the development of a system of generic coding for manuscript preparation that is independent of any particular device and is relatively easy and economical for authors to use. If generic coding succeeds in creating 'a transferable electronic file that can be processed on any machine and used as input for any application in order to increase the productivity of authors and publishers, to permit the use of data in many forms, and to facilitate indexing and cataloging,' it will indeed constitute a major breakthrough.

5.2.3 Optical disc technology

The optical disc is widely viewed as the great technological opportunity for the 1980s. Its enormous potential and technical feasibility have been recognised for many years, but it has had a rather long gestation period owing to the unreliability of equipment, which has alienated consumers and the business community. Now its commercial prospects look brighter.

There are two types of optical discs; both employ lasers for recording and playback, but each is suited to particular tasks. The optical *video* disc has the capacity to handle graphics as well as text, which gives it an advantage over magnetic tape. It also enjoys advantages over videotape: random access and the capacity to combine sound with still frames. So far it has been used primarily for the entertainment market and for training and other industrial and governmental uses. Players and discs developed for industrial users are both different from and more expensive than those for home television because they are formatted to permit random access and to be able to hold a single frame (freeze frame capacity).

The first commercial application of video disc technology for online use was introduced in 1981. It is VIDEO PATSEARCH, which offers access to some 800,000 US patents certified since 1971. The database can now be accessed through the online vendor, BRS, which provides the information necessary for calling up the appropriate text and drawings from one of the video discs supplied by the service, an affiliate of Pergamon International.

Thus far, use of video disc databases by educational and publishing groups has constituted a very small percentage of the market, but the suitability of the video disc for educational and scholarly purposes is very high. It is especially suited to the storage of scientific journals because of its capacity to combine text and graphics. It also has great potential in the medical field, where graphics, colour, and motion sequences are highly important, particularly for microscopic viewing.

The Director of the National Library of Medicine has pointed out that video discs are also eminently suitable for what he called 'prospective preservation', storing information in machine-readable form before deterioration of a printed medium sets in. He estimated that one video disc could store 100,000 pages of text — the annual output of perhaps 100 scientific journals.

The economics of video disc production are not unlike those of book publishing: producing the first copy is very expensive, but additional copies can be produced cheaply. Producing a disc may cost $2,000 to $4,000 per side, but reproducing the disc may cost only $10.

The alternative technology, the optical *digital* disc, is used for computer storage and does not provide the video capacity. Its great attraction is its capacity for mass storage — many times that of magnetic tape — and random access at low cost. Disc storage units may look like jukebox arrangements. One proposal for a disc pack of six doubled discs in a jukebox should have 'the storage capacity of 100 billion characters in the same space now required for a magnetic disc pack with a capacity of 300 million characters.'

5.2.4 Computers in the classroom

Even though there is a general acceptance among educators that computer-assisted instruction (CAI) shows far greater promise than the audio-visual bubble of two decades ago, there still are many imponderables. How much money can and should be spent for this new mode of instruction is a matter of debate — particularly if it must or can be obtained only at the sacrifice of other educational expenditures. The most important consideration is whether, and how soon, quality courseware can be developed, courseware that breaks out of the simple drill exercises which were the first successes in CAI. The lack of satisfactory courseware is the big lament of educators and publishers. The challenge to the scholarly community is to make sure that the substance and the processes embodied in the courseware developed in the years ahead truly add a dimension to instruction that is not now present.

If the computer takes hold as an instructional tool — and it has been called 'the textbook of the next decade ' — the potential market will be enormous. A projection prepared for the National Institute of Education indicated that if a goal were set of 30 minutes a day of interactive computer time for each of the USA's 40 million students, the schools would need 4 million computer units, and to reach that goal by 1990 would require a 50% a year increase in purchases. Thereafter, maintenance and replacement costs would keep the industry busy. The demand for courseware to fill those 30 minutes a day for 12 years of a pupil's education would be enormous. Such aggregate costs are useful for defining the future of the industry, but on a per-pupil basis the costs are modest — an estimated $1 \cdot 2\%$ of the instructional budget.

Thus, unless there is a sudden and wholly unexpected disillusionment with computers in the classroom, the next generation of college students will be highly skilled in the use of the technology, and eventually there will be a considerable impact on scholarly communication.

Nevertheless, despite the momentum of technological development and the expanding market for microcomputers, the prospect for computers in college classrooms is more uncertain than for lower grades because very little courseware exists and most of what is available is not good. It has been argued that until the educational market is bigger, it will not pay software manufacturers to invest in courseware development, and until courseware is developed computers will not be bought for instruction. But the boom in home computer sales may help break the stalemate. Sales in early 1983 were running at twice sales for 1982, and by 1985 there may be 10 million sets in use.

A recent study of the state of courseware cited a number of reasons for the failures to date: there is a big gap between the state of the art and what is being offered. Publishers of courseware do not appreciate the powerful possibilities of the medium, which have been demonstrated by experts, and researchers need to do a better job of making known the results of their experiments. Producing a course of study requires the collaboration of persons with many skills: subject matter experts, imaginative programmers, and teachers. Similarly, there is need for cooperation among different levels of government in the educational process. Some states have done exceptionally good work, the Minnesota Education Computer Consortium often being cited, and so have some local school boards. But there is a federal role, too, particularly in financing research. In addition, scholars from all disciplines must be drawn into the effort to work with government, to collaborate with publishers, to test materials, and to make known their evaluations of what is available and what needs to be done.

5.2.5 Feasibility versus acceptance

The feasibility of a new technological application is no assurance that a proposed change is needed or wanted — a rather obvious point that sometimes is overlooked.

A decade ago, for example, when there was great concern about the proliferation of journals, rising costs, and the burden being placed on researchers and libraries to keep up with the flood of material, there were numerous experiments with alternatives to the conventional journal. One of the more ambitious and interesting was undertaken by the Institute of Electrical and Electronics Engineers (IEEE). The IEEE introduced a new service for its members, the *Annals of the IEEE* which offered a customised service to keep IEEE members apprised of the contents of all the IEEE's 37 journals. In addition to the one journal that came with payment of dues, a member could obtain automatically a reprint of articles in his or her field of interest. The match between a member's interests and the contents of the journals was achieved through the preparation of an interest profile of the member and descriptions of the contents of the annual output of 3,000 articles.

With the support of the National Science Foundation (NSF), which invested heavily in problems of scientific communication in the 1970s, the IEEE spent two years perfecting and testing reader profiles and the matching system. Readers could specify not only the subjects that interested them but also the intensity of their interest and their preference for theoretical or applied material. An exclusion feature made it possible to prevent duplication of material that had already been obtained by subscription to one or more IEEE journals.

When the *Annals* was first offered to the membership after two years of experimentation, it included a less expensive option — a list of relevant articles rather than the reprints themselves.

The membership of the IEEE was 170,000, and only a 1% favourable response was needed, but the response was only one-tenth of that target (200 subscribers) and only 35 of them elected to obtain reprints; most subscribers were primarily interested in improving their current awareness of the literature rather than collecting the reprints.

Follow-up studies showed that the subscribers were enthusiastic (the renewal rate was 97%) but they also gave some clues about why 99.9% of the members were not more receptive. First, the average IEEE member then paid about $20 a year for professional literature, beyond the $45 annual dues which included one journal, and had no intention of spending more. The existing system was cheaper; journal literature was widely available through libraries and companies, and the perception of a crisis resulting from the proliferation of journal literature faded away. These attitudes might well have been detected in advance if the same ingenuity and thoroughness that characterised the technical testing of the proposal had been applied to a marketing analysis.

A decade later, the online database systems are making possible far more extensive customised searches of current literature in a much more convenient fashion. New bibliographies and full text of articles are being continually introduced, particularly in the sciences and business where timeliness is of particular importance. The American Chemical Society's decision to offer online access to the full text of its 18 journals on 1 June 1983 is a recent example. The system had been tested for three years with samples of chemists to determine their information-seeking behaviour, how frequently they used the system, how much time they spent in each session, and what they looked for. The reception among users during the trial period was uniformly enthusiastic, but the question of how many will be willing to pay for the service remains to be answered. Full text may prove to be largely a better search device for the immediate future, its full potential remaining unrealised until optical video discs become part of the online system, so that graphic materials and tables can be included. An ambitious plan of a group of American and British journal publishers to provide electronic services — ADONIS — was recently abandoned owing, presumably, to uncertainty over its financial prospects. As competition stiffens among database vendors, one wonders whether this industry, like the microcomputer industry, faces a shake-out. Meanwhile, the industry shows great vitality.

5.2.6 Technology and the humanities

In the foregoing discussion, no attempt has been made to view the humanities as a distinctive problem, though there are obvious differences among fields in the importance of timeliness, in the magnitude of the advantages conferred by computer capacity, and in the way scholars work. On some matters it is very difficult to assess the relevance of new technology for one field as opposed to another. On some questions it does not matter. One might speculate, for example, that computers are as suitable for bibliographic searches in the humanities as in the social sciences or sciences, but that, in general, the computer is less likely to be essential for major achievements in the humanities than in the sciences. The computer is indispensable in the sciences, but only a useful adjunct to research in the humanities. Or, one might concede that the computer is better for some tasks than others, but the distinguishing factor is the task, not the discipline.

A leading social scientist and university administrator recently argued, in another context, that the distinction between research in the humanities and sciences has been exaggerated. He said that humanists (including the authors of the report of the Commission on the Humanities) have failed to emphasise sufficiently the value of humanistic research and its basic similarity to research in other fields. He deplored the tendency to differentiate it from research in the sciences by calling it 'scholarly activity' or 'scholarly contributions' — with the further implication that it is undertaken for private satisfaction and adds little to the community. His argument rested in part on the failure to appreciate the highly subjective nature of much scientific research. If he is correct, one is led to view research as a continuum covering all fields, with gradations in the importance of empirical techniques or subjective reasoning — a perspective that may be equally appropriate in assessing computer technology.

On the other hand there is a deep worry within the humanistic community about the misapplications of computer technology. As expressed in a recent issue of *Daedalus,* the fear is not that directories and reference publications will go out of fashion, but that 'we will increasingly think of knowledge as information, exulting in our new databanks where we ought to be examining critically the hypotheses we fashion. The existence of vastly improved technology for rapid transmission of information raises fundamental questions about what kinds of information are worth securing and about whether information is indeed our chief lack.' The fear may be justified, but the mistaking of information for knowledge is hardly new, nor is the failure to examine hypotheses critically. Computer technology may happen to heighten the visibility of the concern, but that it introduces a new problem is not self-evident.

The report of the Commission on the Humanities does give considerable attention to the role of computers and, properly, puts great emphasis on managing the applications of information technology. This includes harnessing its power to advance humanistic scholarship and influencing the way it is worked into the education curriculum and home environment. Irrespective of how scholars use computers in their own work, they should have a great deal to say about how the computer is integrated into everyday life. To be effective in this role, they need to have a full understanding of the technology. They need to read about what is happening, the implications of what is happening, and the policy issues posed by technological changes. One can argue that they must go farther. They need to acquire the 'hands-on' experience that comes with using computers at work and in the home. Then they will be better prepared to speak out on applications and implications. The pervasiveness and power of computer technology argues for giving it special attention, not merely as a tool of scholarly communication but as a force in economic and social development.

5.3 Traditional concerns

Although an Office of Scholarly Communication and Technology would be particularly concerned with problems related to technological changes, it would also be concerned with such traditional issues as managerial efficiency, the impact of government on higher education, copyright, peer review and the publishing policies of scholarly journals. These matters are discussed below.

5.3.1 Collaboration and other managerial issues

The advantages of collaborative arrangements in publishing, stressed in the Enquiry report, have been confirmed over the past four or five years. An increasing number of presses and societies are now producing services jointly or obtaining them from larger organisations that can provide them more efficiently.

Heldref, which was established in Washington more than a decade ago to provide a protective umbrella over scholarly periodicals that were struggling for survival, doubled the number of its journals from 20 to 40. Annual revenues increased from about $1 million to more than $2 million. With expansion came funds for converting a rather simple strike-on composition facility to a computerised photocomposition operation. After a year's transition, the new technology not only proved financially advantageous but contributed to a better product and increased the satisfaction of the Heldref clients. Eighteen of the 40 journals are losing money, but they can be kept alive because the others generate enough additional revenue to carry the losers and to permit the build-up of a fund to cover subscription liability and to increase operating funds. Small declines in circulation have been suffered by several journals, but marketing efforts have been strengthened to help gain back subscribers.

The JHUP, which was an innovative force in providing a variety of services to university presses and other scholarly non-profit publishers, has increased the number of participants in its consortium from 10 in 1977 to 20. All members of the consortium get data-processing services and are free to choose other services that are available, including credit management, warehousing, and shipping.

The consortium organised by the MLA has also grown in the past few years. By early 1983, 18 organisations were obtaining membership and financial services provided by the MLA computer system. Some of them have also called on MLA to produce directories. Photo-typesetter services will probably be offered to consortium members in 1984 if the plans to start preparing camera-ready copy in-house for the MLA's journal, *PMLA*, at the beginning of 1984 work out satisfactorily. The American Anthropological Association (AAA), which has provided membership and publishing services for other anthropological societies, has proposed an expansion that would bring AAA together with other large societies in the ACLS. Grants from the Mellon Foundation, administered by the ACLS, encouraged additional collaborative efforts in the early 1980s.

Meanwhile, a commercial firm entered the field. Harper & Row began offering fulfilment services to non-profit publishers and now counts university presses among its clients. Harper handles fulfilment and warehousing for a half-dozen such presses, primarily in the Midwest, and has succeeded in upgrading service to customers and reducing costs 'beyond expectation', according to one director. It will also handle foreign marketing and distribution for some of the presses. The arrangement requires the presses to adjust to Harper procedures, but at the same time reduces headaches.

Cooperative ventures have not been limited to warehousing and financial operations. The Southeastern University Press Marketing Group, set up as an outgrowth of a planning meeting financed by an ACLS grant, is now planning its third year of activity. The group has cooperatively financed the hiring of a sales representative who covers the South-East twice a year for the 10 member presses. Further marketing cooperative ventures are also under consideration, including arrangements for clearance sales of member-press books on the respective campuses.

Another modest proposal for collaboration, which has considerable promise for cost-saving and efficiency, has been made by the University Press of New England and several others to establish a computerised book review list that is kept up to date and provides breakdowns by fields of interest, type of readership, and so on. For a single medium-sized press, the savings are likely to be six to eight weeks' time of a staff member.

There has now been enough experience with collaborative arrangements and with the purchase of fulfilment and financial services from large presses to remove any doubts about the advantages for small organisations that are operating on an inefficient scale. The ACLS office could play a helpful role in getting the word to small publishers and societies that are still going it alone at considerable sacrifice.

The attempt to increase efficiency through collaboration, which gained momentum during the late 1970s, is part of the broader, and never-ending problem of cutting costs. Directors of learned societies and publishers are continually on the lookout for new technology that will save money over the long run and for suppliers who are offering better prices without a serious reduction in service. By and large, informal exchanges of information and meetings, such as those of the ACLS secretaries and the AAUP, are probably sufficient. But a new office should be alert to the possibility that it may be able to find some useful role to play in gathering and disseminating information related to such managerial aspects of publishing.

Similarly, there is continuing concern about ways to increase revenues. Learned societies, caught between rising costs and the fear of alienating members by raising dues, have faced a tightening financial squeeze. The National Enquiry attributed much of the financial difficulty of many journals to their failure to raise subscription prices or dues adequately, and there appears to be considerable difference in the success of different publishers in persuading their readers to accept a realistic price policy. More information about subscribers' responses to price increases — and how to cope with them — seems highly desirable.

Other responses to the squeeze have varied. One strategy has been to unbundle the package of services given to members; for example, charging separately for publications that were formerly included in the dues package. Another has been to reduce dependence on dues as the principal source of income by developing other sources of revenue — providing services to smaller societies, developing bibliographies or abstract services for sale, actively seeking outside grants for special projects, promoting advertising revenue, and, to a much lesser extent, imposing special charges, such as submission fees. The submission fee, which has been introduced by many social science publications, has faced strong opposition in the humanities where editors believe it would offend authors or that, at best, it would bring in so little additional revenue as to constitute a nuisance. The attractiveness of the pay-off clearly varies, depending on the size of a publication's manuscript-reading burden, the total cost of the publishing, and the size of the fee that could be imposed. Those who support the fee cite not only the income, but also its effect on submission practices: payment of a fee is likely to encourage authors to choose more carefully the journals to which they send their work, thereby reducing the burden of review. Some journals pass the fee to reviewers.

Much less attention appears to have been devoted to revenue-raising issues than to cost-cutting ones, and if this inference is correct it suggests that the proposed office might take the lead in encouraging appropriate groups to conduct a workshop on the topic.

5.3.2 Government policies

Some government policies affect scholarly communication directly — changes in postal rates, for example, or funding of research, funding of library operations, subsidies for exports, and copyright laws. Other policies affect scholarly communication less directly such as expenditures for higher education, tax treatment of investment in technology, tax treatment of charitable contributions, laws discriminating against imports. Even broad economic policies that are intended to speed up economic activity, or reduce inflation, have an impact. In a period of inflation, for example, educational institutions have a more difficult job passing along higher costs than do profit-making businesses. Institutions heavily dependent on endowment income are hurt in periods when the purchasing power of fixed investments declines. In general, higher education and scholarly communication are subject to the same forces that affect the entire economy, as well as to a wide range of special governmental actions.

An instructive example of the effects of postal rate changes on journal publishing appeared in *Scholarly Publishing*. Between 1976 and 1982 in the UK, postal rates for publications were raised about 25% faster than the general rate of inflation. Postage, which had been an almost negligible consideration for journal publishers, moved up toward a level of 10% of total costs. The financial impact forced a number of weaker periodicals to take defensive measures, including: reducing frequency of publication, reducing the number of pages in each issue (the step most frequently cited, having been taken by more than 20% of the journals responding to the survey), shifting to microfiche publication, reducing the weight of paper, and combining journals. A few even decided to publish abroad because British rates for international mail rose proportionately more rapidly than those for domestic mail. There was no mention of online publishing or on-demand publishing as alternatives.

The scholarly community cannot typically expect more favourable treatment than other users, but it can at least try to make its voice heard when it appears to be bearing a disproportionate burden.

The higher education, publishing, and library communities have long been staffed to monitor the major, continuing legislative areas, such as postal and copyright changes, but from time to time emergencies arise or new problem areas emerge that require fresh responses. The early 1980s were such a time, and two organisations were started by the social scientists and humanists in response to threats of heavy budget cuts. They are the Consortium of Social Science Associations (COSSA) and the NHA. Both seem to have developed a long-run role despite the *ad hoc* nature of their original founding.

COSSA, which traces its origins back to the early 1970s, established a Washington office in 1981 when the NSF and other research and educational institutes faced severe funding cutbacks. COSSA was supported primarily by funds from the major social science organisations. After an initial three-month trial and a brief extension, it achieved permanent status and formally incorporated in June 1982. COSSA has four major activities, including lobbying and communication among social scientists through a weekly newsletter that reaches an audience of 650. The letter deals mostly with legislative issues.

The NHA was established early in 1981 when it became apparent that there was no organised constituency to speak up for the NEH, then threatened by a 50% cut in its appropriations. Most of the initial funding came from ACLS and its constituent societies, with additional support from the American Association of Higher Education, the AAUP, and others.

The NHA is essentially a lobbying organisation, working with congressional staff to prepare testimony, and rounding up witnesses for hearings. It issues a monthly newsletter for its supporting organisations and handles requests for information from members.

Unlike COSSA, which deals with issues affecting the social science community through government, the NHA focuses exclusively on NEH. The NHA has considered the alternative of becoming involved in other issues, but has decided to keep its exclusive focus because this is where the need is greatest.

COSSA and the NHA appear to be performing an important role in the scholarly community's extensive lobbying effort, and they are potentially useful sources of information on government activities and legislation for the proposed ACLS office.

5.3.3 Copyright issues

Copyright, a vast and complicated subject, already commands the attention of specialists representing publishers, authors, libraries and other interested parties. There is no need for additional partisan representation in continuing controversies. However, some of the knottiest copyright issues are related to higher education and scholarly communication; for example, copying of material for class use and protection of data in electronic systems, and so the subject cannot be ignored by an organisation trying to answer questions about scholarly communication. As a minimum, an Office should be able to refer a questioner to helpful people at the Copyright Office, the AAP, and others. The Office should be acquainted with basic sources of information such as documents from the Copyright Office and the bimonthly *Copyright Law Reporter*, produced by the Commerce Clearinghouse.

An issue that has attracted special attention in recent years — the copying of copyrighted material for course use on college campuses across the USA — came to a head with the filing of a suit by nine publishers against New York University, 10 of its faculty members, and a photocopying shop near campus. The suit was settled out of court with an agreement calling for discontinuation of excessive copying. It provided no precise legal guidelines for the future, however, and has created some uncertainty, but it may have achieved its intended effect. Some observers believe that professors accustomed to reproducing quantities of material for class use are more sensitive to copyright issues and that gross violations of the copyright law have been reduced. The leading chain of copying services has reported a drop in sales of some 20-30%. Universities are taking a long look at the problem to make sure that their policies are appropriate, and revising them where they are not. Drafts of new policy guides are being circulated for comment on campuses: advice is being sought.

The ARL has, however, expressed some reservations about this trend. It fears that the out-of-court agreement (and the report of the Copyright Office described below) may lead to an unnecessarily restrictive view of fair use that would inhibit scholarly research and communication.

Another important issue has been the balancing of the rights of creators and the needs of users of copyrighted works held in libraries and archives. Section 108 of the copyright law requires the US Copyright Office to report every five years on the photocopying practices of libraries and their clients. The first report, delivered to the Congress in January 1983, found that the present law provides the framework for achieving balance between creators and users but that in practice it has not always adequately protected publishers' needs. For example, questionable multiple photocopying was detected. Librarians tended to see the report, overall, as a vindication of their view that the present law is working; publishers, on the other hand, saw it as evidence that the system is seriously flawed. The report to Congress included a list of recommendations made to the Office to improve understanding of the present system and to clarify ambiguities in the statute. Further debate on these matters can be expected since important differences of view persist.

Other copyright issues of emerging or current concern include the protection of material on optical discs, protection of software embodied in microchips, and the protection of material that is being shown online — all questions related to recent technological innovations. The Copyright Office itself has not gone untouched by the new technology. On 1 October 1982, it ended manual filing of copyright registrations. Registrations since 1 January 1978, are accessible online. For the 1866-1978 period the original catalogue cards are still in use — 41 million of them.

Meanwhile, the Copyright Clearance Center reports considerable progress in its effort to systematise and simplify the use of copyrighted materials and the compensation of copyright owners. The Enquiry had recommended strongly that journals, libraries, and scholars cooperate in making the Center work (Recommendation 6). It is apparent that users and producers have responded to the Center's efforts to increase its effectiveness; participation in its payment system has increased steadily, as have revenues, despite the ease with which the law can be ignored and the nuisance cost of compliance with the present system.

From 1978 to 1982 the Center collected $1·7 million in royalty fees, a modest sum, but it is increasing every year. During 1982 alone, fees totalled $615,000 and for 1983 they were running about 40% ahead of the preceding year. Corporate payments rose noticeably following the out-of-court settlement of a suit for copyright infringement brought against two firms by the AAP. Most of the royalties have been paid to scientific publishers, including three major professional associations, the American Chemical Society, the American Institute of Physics, and the IEEE.

Participation in the Center's programme has also increased. Some 700 publishers have joined, compared with 200 in 1979. The number of publications has risen to 6,600, including newsletters, magazines, and books (primarily reference works and computer books), in addition to the technical, scientific, and professional journals that accounted for most of the initial list of participants. The number of participating libraries has stabilised at about 1,500, compared with 800 in 1979.

To cope with the nuisance problem, the Copyright Clearance Center devised an Annualized Authorization payment system which will enable corporate users of copyrighted material to pay a fee for unlimited use. The fee is based on a 90-day audit of copying. The audit is intended to establish the basis of the fee and the sharing of receipts among copyright holders. The new system is a response to users who have claimed that their objection is not to the payment of fees, which they have said they are quite willing to make, but rather to the transaction costs of complying with the present system. It may not solve the needs of all users, and for publishers who do participate in the Center's programme the situation remains unchanged, but there is clear evidence of progress. Much remains to be learned about the relative importance of the Center's work. The statistics cited are only a beginning, and a broader study might be within the proposed Office's purview.

5.3.4 Other concerns

A number of issues raised during the course of the National Enquiry may be re-examined from time to time to see whether they merit exploration or comment. These include peer review, and the scholar's need for comprehensive and up-to-date information on submission of manuscripts.

Peer review continues to be a lively subject in debates over manuscript evaluation and, among scientists, in grant-giving as well. The practice is well-entrenched, and even its critics generally concede that it is probably indispensable, even if flawed; it gives credibility to the editorial process, allaying suspicions of favouritism and prejudice; it increases the likelihood that trivial material will not be printed; and when the system is effective it leads to the publication of better manuscripts.

According to its defenders, the topic remains controversial partly because it is misunderstood. For example, the fact that referees disagree does not mean that the system is wrong, it merely reflects honest differences in judgment. That the system is not perfect is no argument for abandoning it unless something better is put in its place. A few critics would prefer to let everything be published and leave to the individual scholar the task of differentiating good from bad.

There is disagreement over the question of whether a scholar with a proven research record should be given a higher rating by journal referees than a scholar with a poor record, or whether the quality of the manuscript itself should be all that matters.

The advantages of blind submissions (that is, manuscripts submitted for review without the author's name attached) continue to be debated. Some scholars refuse to serve as a journal referee unless the author is identified. Similarly, there are differences over whether the names of the referees should be divulged to the scholar. An editor who recently reported on a five-year experiment with blind reviewing — which he thought had proved to be considerably superior to the practice it replaced — said there had been a detectable increase in the proportion of manuscripts accepted from assistant professors, women, scholars outside the North-East corridor, and authors without university affiliation during the five-year period. He acknowledged, however, that it is not incontrovertibly clear that this finding could be attributed solely to a change in the method of peer review. Further exchanges of information about similar experiences might well be encouraged by the proposed Office.

Among the early groups that offered information about the market for scholarly manuscripts were the American Philosophical Association and the MLA. Since that time guides have been prepared for other disciplines, among them *Political science journal information*, published in 1982 by the American Political Science Association. It is a definitive listing of scholarly journals for political scientists and of the review and publication procedures they follow. Data, obtained by questionnaire, are provided for 52 journals (about four out of five of those to whom the questionnaires were sent).

In addition to the individual journal reports, the publication includes a summary of the data, which many authors will find instructive. It shows that: acceptance rates average about 20%; the preferred article length is 20 to 30 pages; three out of five journal editors are now soliciting articles; the review process usually takes about two and a half months; the elapsed time from submission to publication is typically a year; and so on. Such averages obscure a wide variety of review and publication practices. The preferred editorial style also varies widely; there is no one guide that, if followed, would make a manuscript acceptable in style to most publications.

There is room both for guides in other disciplines and for a synthesis and analysis of data from the various directories. But, piece by piece, information is being assembled that provides a useful perspective on scholarly publishing.

5.4 Establishing an Office of Scholarly Communication and Technology

What would an Office of Scholarly Communication and Technology do and how would it operate? The definitive answers to both questions will emerge from experience, but from previous studies a number of functions and activities can readily be identified. Since there is much more to be done than can possibly be started at once, the agenda will have to be selective. Initially at least, the office should serve more as a catalyst than a doer — stimulating and coordinating projects rather than conducting them — though the distinction may at times become blurred. In the long run the opportunity exists for a very broad and ambitious programme.

5.4.1 Functions and activities

The activities of a new office can be grouped under five major functions: (1) disseminating information through clearing-house and reference services; (2) monitoring statistics on publishing, library, and related activities and encouraging development of better data; (3) improving liaison among groups that make up the scholarly communication system; (4) promoting educational activities (especially with regard to new technology) among groups in the system; and (5) directing or encouraging special studies of how the system is working.

1. Information clearing-house, reference service, and newsletter. At the present time, keeping up with what is happening in the field of scholarly communication means keeping up with a large number of very different activities:

— with what is happening in libraries, as reported in the *Bowker Annual* and *Library Journal, Online, Database,* the newsletter of the ARL and the ARL's *Proceedings,* the annual report of the CLR, and reports of the studies it commissions;

— with what is happening in publishing, as reported in *Publishers Weekly, Scholarly Publishing,* the newsletter of the AAUP, and reports from the AAP;

— with what is happening in the field of higher education, as reported in the *Chronicle of Higher Education* and publications issued by Knowledge Industries, and *Computers and the Humanities;*

— with what is happening in the foundation world, as reported in *Foundation News,* published by the Council on Foundations;

— with what is happening in government, as reflected in *Humanities* (the publication of the NEH), the annual report of the NSF (as well as special NSF studies), Copyright Office reports, and the newsletters issued by the activist organisations, the COSSA, and the NHA;

— with what is happening in technology, as reflected in *Science* magazine and such trade publications as *Information Hotline.*

This listing, which is illustrative rather than exhaustive, indicates the range of information sources that produce material relevant to understanding what is happening in the field of scholarly communication.

A logical function of the new Office would be to serve as a clearing-house of information generated by different organisations for their own purposes or for subscribers but that is also of concern to others. Such an activity logically begins with assembling a modest library of a dozen or more newsletters and magazines, and a collection of key reference books and important reports. (Eventually, a terminal should be installed capable of searching databases of concern to humanists and social scientists.) This collection would serve a dual purpose. First, it would be the backbone of a reference service that could respond to inquiries, either by providing information or by directing the caller or letter writer to another information source (preferably an individual rather than an organisation). To be effective, this reference service should establish a directory of information sources, ideally on the computer for easy access.

Secondly, the library would be a major source of information for a new newsletter or a service to existing newsletters. Flexible in timing and size, a newsletter can be produced easily and quickly, and distributed inexpensively. However, newsletters have proliferated as rapidly as journals, and any proposal to start another one requires close scrutiny.

ACLS constituent societies and many organisations serving groups within the scholarly communications system have their own newsletters, but these publications either give little attention to scholarly communication or else concentrate on one particular aspect of it. No single newsletter adequately reaches representatives of all these groups or stresses common concerns among publishers, librarians, scholars, and educators interested in new technology. A serious newsletter covering issues identified in this report would not be duplicative.

Three variations on the newsletter approach can be readily defined. First, a new publication could be produced by the ACLS Office, emphasising technological developments affecting scholarly communication but including notes on the traditional concerns discussed earlier in this report. Determining the contents might pose less of a problem than would distribution. Who would receive the newsletter? Would they receive it free or by paid subscription? Starting a newsletter is not difficult, but producing an effective one requires a great deal of thought and planning.

A second, less costly alternative would be to supply information to existing newsletters — either as camera-ready copy, or as a manuscript that could easily be adapted to an editor's needs. This material could be incorporated in an existing newsletter or attached as a self-contained supplement. (Additional supplementary distribution of such material could also be made by ACLS to a selected subset of its own mailing list.)

Finally, the ACLS newsletter itself could be expanded. For example, each issue could contain a section devoted to scholarly communication. If this approach were taken, it would have to be accompanied by a careful study of the existing ACLS mailing list to judge whether its coverage is appropriate, whether it needs to be expanded, or whether a supplementary distribution list would have to be developed if the decision were made to incorporate all scholarly communication information in a single issue. This approach implies a thorough re-examination of the ACLS newsletter — its purpose, content, and format.

The strongest argument for a newsletter is that it would contribute directly to the process of scholarly communication by disseminating useful information. It could help draw together a group of readers with a commitment to scholarly communication.

2. *Monitoring and data development.* The principal purpose of an Office of Scholarly Communication, as envisioned by the National Enquiry (Recommendation 11), was monitoring trends in book and journal publishing and in library operations and use. The proposed

ACLS Office would also have a monitoring responsibility, but it would be broader; it would cover not only publishing and library trends, but also trends in the application of new technology to teaching and research.

Monitoring would entail keeping up with results of special studies and the data series now maintained by commercial firms such as RR Bowker, by professional and business trade associations such as the AAP and the ARL, or by governmental agencies such as the LC. It would not include gathering primary statistical data, which is an enormously expensive and difficult enterprise.

Nevertheless, the monitoring role should not be merely passive. It should include an effort to persuade producers of statistical information to revise their tabulations, to expand their work, or to make special computer runs to provide information that can be more useful to the scholarly community.

Available data on publishing and library operations have been subject to considerable criticism with regard both to scope and validity — they are particularly inadequate for assessing the state of scholarly communication. With rare exceptions, such as some AAUP surveys, data on such elementary matters as number of titles published, price changes, proliferation of journals, and so on are open to one or more of the following shortcomings:

> no distinction is made in the data between scholarly and non-scholarly works;

> breakdowns by discipline are either missing or are archaic and meaningless;

> findings for small samples are published without any indication of whether they are representative of the larger universe;

> time spans are limited; much of the most useful data are available only from special studies covering a single year or a few years, with no likelihood of being updated.

The likelihood of any easy solution to these and other shortcomings is remote. Fritz Machlup's efforts in the late 1970s demonstrated clearly the cost and difficulty of the task. His report, *Information through the printed word*, makes incontrovertibly clear the glaring weaknesses of available data and the obstacles to the production of satisfactory statistics. Modest improvements and additions to data are feasible, however, and they are worth pursuing with data producers. For example, the LC could be asked to explore the feasibility of including in its cataloguing database a designation of books that are considered scholarly. Compilations of separate statistics on scholarly books would then be possible. Similarly, statistics on periodicals could be developed that distinguished among scholarly journals, and professional and trade publications and other serials.

The LC could also be asked to provide special statistical compilations of selected data already in its computer files. It did provide such a pilot test more than three years ago in a report prepared for the NEH. Tabulations obtained from the LC at little cost made it possible to prepare charts comparing the number of new serials introduced in the social sciences and in the humanities between 1972 and 1979 by discipline. The pattern of growth was similar in both areas, peaking in the mid-1970s and then tapering off. About three times as many new serials were introduced in the social sciences as in the humanities.

Historically, the LC has not provided statistical summaries of its activities, but the computerisation of its records clearly makes it capable of doing so, and the cost need not be burdensome.

Another pilot effort, prepared for the NEH study, was carried out by the MLA. It demonstrated the feasibility of developing statistical series from databases prepared for other purposes. As a spin-off of its *International bibliography,* the MLA obtains a list of all periodicals publishing articles in its fields of interest and sends the editor of each one a questionnaire requesting information on those facts of publication likely to be of interest to potential authors, readers, and librarians. A database prepared from these is used to prepare the biennial *Directory of periodicals.* Four years ago, a program was written for this database, which produced a profile of language journals, including the following characteristics:

Frequency of publication — roughly half of the periodicals are published three or four times a year.

Proliferation of journals and serials — three times as many new periodicals were started during the 1965-1974 decade as during the 1945-1954 decade.

Circulation — 40% have fewer than 1,000 subscribers.

Elapsed time between submission of an article and the publication decision — less than two months for 45% of the journals; more than four months for 16%.

Elapsed time between publication decision and publication of an article — more than one year for 25% of the journals.

Monitoring trends in new technology will be very difficult, though it may also prove to be of greater interest. The area of particular attention now — microcomputers — is a new one, and there seems to be no established statistical system to gather sales data on models, prices, use, and so on. It is also changing rapidly. There have been special reports, but it is difficult to piece together consistent numbers that show growth and change. The National Center for Educational Statistics recently produced an estimate of the number of computers in public schools in the USA (about 120,000 in 1982, double the number reported in the preceding year), but a systematic programme for getting up-to-date, reliable information about the number and kinds of computers, their locations, the purposes for which they are used by how many students, and with what effect, does not yet exist.

In addition, it is difficult to discover how much R&D money is going into the development of computer hardware, software, and courseware in the humanities. The identification of reliable sources of such information will present a major challenge to the Office.

Numbers on the spread of online cataloguing in libraries are encountered frequently, but a reliable set of statistics does not seem to be available.

Since there is no end to the things that can be counted, the Office will have to give particular attention to selecting monitoring activities that not only are important today, but are likely to be of increasing importance five or ten years from now. It will have to allocate its monitoring resources between selecting the best and most useful available data, and stimulating cooperative efforts with data producers to encourage the collection of better information and new data — both with an eye to the question, 'Who wants these statistics, for what purpose, and with how much real need?'

3. Liaison. A central theme of the National Enquiry, and one that recurs continually, is the need to improve personal communication among publishers, librarians, and other scholars. A member of the board of the Enquiry cited the exchange of information among representatives of these different sectors of the system as a major contribution of the Enquiry. The board members, at least, were able to enrich their understanding, and one can surmise that exposing others to a similar experience would be equally beneficial. There is no dearth of experts in particular specialities, but relatively few people have a perspective that encompasses the whole system. The ACLS Committee on Scholarly Communication has been one effort to keep discussions going among representatives of different sectors. The growth of the Society for Scholarly Publishing has been another, and there have been many informal meetings among individuals who have come to know each other through these activities. While these activities continue, new ways to promote better liaison among the sectors of the scholarly communication system should be explored.

One unexploited opportunity for promoting understanding among various groups exists on the campuses. To date, scholarly communication as an identifiable problem has been discussed by leaders in the publishing and library fields, and by a number of the learned societies. Occasionally, it has been placed on the agenda of annual meetings. Specific aspects of the problem (from printing costs, to refereeing, to new technology) have been addressed by the professionals in a field. But scholarly communication as a campus-wide problem (like the budget or admissions policies) has not been addressed. This is probably an oversight, for the campus perspective offers possibilities that may not be realisable through other approaches.

Annual — or more frequent — meetings or workshops could be developed which would bring together the university librarian, the university press director (if there is a press on campus), the computer centre director, any journal editors on campus, and scholars from any discipline who are especially interested in the dissemination of knowledge. Such a workshop would have to be planned carefully in order to focus on problems in which the participants had a common interest — new technologies affecting library services, for example, or changes in government policies affecting the communication of knowledge. The agenda would encourage the sharing of information about the potential usefulness of technological changes as well as about the difficulties they may create. Formal meetings may well lead to an increase in informal exchanges. Such sessions would help the campus community understand the nature of changes underway in services or policies that affect it, and would enable administrators to get additional feedback on faculty attitudes. Representatives of the system of scholarly communication who also are members of the same campus community should find mutual discussions especially worthwhile, since many decisions affecting scholarly communication for an individual scholar are taken within the boundaries of a single university.

Whether this proposal has merit could readily and inexpensively be tested by sponsoring a few one-day workshops at campuses where one or more faculty members have a strong interest in scholarly communication (Johns Hopkins, Princeton, Columbia, and Minnesota come to mind, among others).

94

The role of the ACLS would be to initiate the project and explore suitable topics in collaboration with appropriate faculty members and then to propose it officially in a letter from the president of ACLS to the president or provost of the host university. The letter would stress the importance of the experiment and the probable benefits to the university. ACLS might offer to underwrite the costs of a luncheon and the expenses entailed in bringing in at least one distinguished outside speaker or discussion leader.

The campus is a community with a set of common interests centred around the university's welfare. It provides an economical and convenient base. Workshops could be conducted at minimal cost. The likelihood that they would be instructive and would lead to new relationships on campus may well be greater than that of more expensive and ambitious efforts.

The need to improve communication among the various disciplines also exists. Although lip service has long been given to interdisciplinary research, the gap among disciplines remains great. Indeed, even within disciplines there is some evidence that the drive toward increasing specialisation has weakened the bonds among scholars. The executive secretary of one association that has lost membership in recent years attributes the loss, in part, to precisely this narrowing focus. Given the rising costs of memberships and publications, some scholars have chosen to support their special discipline and to discontinue membership in their larger society. If this is indeed true, it is not only a problem for individual learned societies, but also for scholarly communication and for the whole enterprise of higher education and scholarship.

Another gap that caused concern and discussion within the board of the National Enquiry, and one that drew attention in the Rockfeller report on the humanities, was dramatised effectively by Maynard Mack's lecture which opened the 1983 meeting of the ACLS in New York. That is the gap between humanist scholars and the general public. If public appreciation of the humanities and support for humanist scholarship is weakening, scholars themselves must share the blame. Notwithstanding the rapid pace of social change, economic pressures, and world tensions commonly cited as factors weakening the commitment to humanistic studies, some part of the problem must be attributable to the narrowness of much humanist scholarship and its remoteness from everyday life.

The proposed ACLS Office should keep on its agenda the question of what to do to improve the links among scholars in different disciplines and between the scholars and the general public. It might well convene a group to consider ways to provide incentives to promote communication across these gaps.

4. Workshops and other educational efforts. The proposed ACLS Office should be prepared to assist in planning and financing two types of short workshops or conferences. One would be designed for leaders in publishing, library policy, and higher education who want to explore emerging problem areas or common concerns that are characterised by considerable difference of opinion, or gaps in knowledge. The groups would be small and would draw on one or more outside experts to lead the discussion. The purpose of the discussions would be to clarify issues and differing viewpoints, to identify information needs and alternative approaches to problems, and to consider the consequences of pursuing different policies. No effort would be made to achieve agreement or to take a policy stand, actions more appropriately left to organisations such as COSSA and NHA. In some circumstances such workshops may be conducted more appropriately under the aegis of publishers or libraries, but the Office still may play a useful role in mobilising the effort.

The other type of workshop would be aimed at helping small learned societies — members of the ACLS and others that might be identified (or editors and business managers within such groups) — to increase their capacity to cope with the practical day-to-day problems that confront them. Although the central purpose of the ACLS Office will be to encourage communication among the different sectors of the system, it should also be alert to opportunities to provide guidance and help to constituencies within the system that lack resources and expertise. Some educational efforts of this nature are now conducted by publishing associations, library groups, and the Society for Scholarly Publishing. Thus, efforts would have to be made to avoid duplication. The Office should move in only where there appears to be a gap, and it should rely heavily on members of the outside groups to develop workshop ideas. The kind of workshop supported by the grants from the Committee on Scholarly Communication, which enabled small presses to explore the advantage of consortia and other collaborative efforts, would fall into this category of activity.

5. Special studies of how the system is working. Relatively little information has been reported about the behaviour and attitude of scholars who are served by the system of scholarly communication. Aside from a number of rather narrow studies, the major data source is the National Enquiry, which tried to shed some light on this question

96

by conducting a survey of 8,000 scholars. Half of them received a questionnaire dealing with their experience as readers of scholarly material; the other half received a questionnaire regarding their experience as authors. More than five years have passed since that survey was taken, and it would be instructive now to conduct a similar survey to see what changes have occurred in scholars' reading habits — the journals they read and buy, their library use — and in authors' impressions of pressures to publish, refereeing, and delays in publication. Although the questions asked in a follow-up survey would touch on many of the areas covered in the earlier survey, they would also explore new areas, especially reactions to new technology. A survey conducted at this early stage in the use of microcomputers and word-processing equipment, for example, would provide a base from which to measure the spread of this relatively new technology, its usefulness, and its impact in such areas as online literature searches and changes in the ways scholars use the library. Ideally, a system should be set up for replicating the survey, or parts of it, at two- or three-year intervals.

Survey research, unfortunately, is expensive, especially if the sample size is large enough to permit breakdowns into such categories as discipline and type of institution. Considerable discussion needs to be given to evaluating alternative sample sizes and the trade-offs associated with various levels of detail, and to deciding what is most appropriate.

A survey of scholars is only one way to gain perspective on how well the system is working. Other approaches are worth putting on the agenda, too.

Statistical information about scholars' behaviour and their attitudes can be enriched by case studies of successful implementations of new technology. General reports abound on how the new technologies work, but if humanists and social scientists are to be attracted to an assessment of whether any of these new technologies are going to benefit them, they must be given examples of applications in their own disciplines. The occasional reports that have been made tend to circulate among the converted. Thought should be given to ways in which good case experiences can be elicited systematically. Some possibilities include: encouraging newsletter or journal editors to obtain reports or letters from their readers on successful applications of new technology, funding a conference or workshop where successes and failures are reported and analysed, and providing modest grants to scholars interested in tracking down and evaluating representative experiences that are especially instructive.

A special study could be undertaken to meet a need that has long been recognised — the lack of information on the quality and performance of scholarly journals. Books are reviewed, but journals are not. Is this merely an accident of history, an oversight that cannot be explained, a topic that is too sensitive, or are there substantial reasons for not trying to undertake such an evaluation? In some fields, surveys have been conducted to arrive at a rating of journals, which is a reasonable beginning but falls far short of a serious enquiry into the substance of journal publishing. The ACLS Office would be a logical organisation to plan a workshop to explore the feasibility of a broad programme of journal assessment and alternative ways to conduct it. Papers could be commissioned on evaluating different approaches and on attempting pilot evaluations.

In the conduct of special studies like those described here, the role of the ACLS Office would be to initiate the planning, raise funds, and select the principal investigators. It would not conduct the actual study.

5.4.2 Organisation of the new Office

The initial staffing and financing requirements are estimated briefly as follows. As a minimum, a director and a secretary (perhaps part-time) will be needed to start the Office. Within a year or so, the workload will probably have grown enough to warrant the hiring of a second professional. Further expansion might well be provided initially by part-time scholars with special competence in one or more areas of activity. A full-time staff of three, augmented by part-time help, could be adequate for the short run.

Considerable additional strength can be obtained from an advisory committee composed of representatives of ACLS constituent societies (secretaries and members) and of other groups that share a common concern about scholarly communication. These include the Social Science Research Council (SSRC) (since many members of ACLS are affiliated with SSRC), ARL, CLR, the AAUP, scholars, and leading educators concerned with the subject.

The Office should not be established without assurance of funding for at least five years. Funding will be needed not only for the staff, but for workshops, a newsletter, and other activities.

Establishing an Office of Scholarly Communication would be in line not only with the recommendations of the National Enquiry but with other actions under way. Steps to strengthen the enterprise of scholarly communication have already been taken by individuals and groups within the system.

The CLR, which has strongly endorsed the establishment of an Office of Scholarly Communication, has conducted conferences and sponsored meetings of foundation officials, publishers, and others on the impact of new technologies on the library system.

The ARL recently adopted a five-year plan that identified, as a major objective, the need 'to understand, contribute to, and improve the system of scholarly communication'. The ARL plan cited as its first step the effort to identify and analyse 'information-seeking behavior of scholars and researchers in various disciplines, the use made of different kinds of library materials, trends in publishing (both hard copy and electronics) in different disciplines, policies and trends in research library acquisitions, etc'. The statement concludes with a powerful plea for 'strong liaison and cooperative effort with other concerned groups, including scholarly and higher education organizations'.

The work of the Primary Communications Research Centre at the University of Leicester in the UK has already been cited, as has the more recent establishment of an Office for Humanities Communication at Leicester, under the aegis of the British Library.

The AAUP has published several studies of scholarly communication and has been an active participant in efforts to improve such communication through its meetings and through the individual efforts of many press directors. The Society for Scholarly Publishing has tried to attract to its membership and to its meetings librarians, experts in communications technology, and others with allied interests.

The time seems right for ACLS to move ahead. The establishment of an Office of Scholarly Communication and Technology would have a symbolic effect. Its mere presence would draw attention to the problem and would legitimise scholarly communication as a continuing concern, not merely the subject of an occasional study when a new crisis is feared. Such less tangible benefits would complement the direct achievements — improvement in information gathering, the success of a newsletter, and the effectiveness of particular workshops and special studies.

6 Recent British initiatives

Since the conference at Cawthorpe House — and probably because of it — there has been an undoubted quickening in the UK in the pace at which research into humanities communication is progressing. This is not to deny the contribution of the previous years. For example, the work of the BLR&D Department has included the area of the arts and humanities since the Gregynog seminar of 1975[1], which called for a programme of research and underlined some themes for future exploration. The progress achieved in the following years was subjected to scrutiny by a seminar held at Sheffield in March 1980, the proceedings of which were subsequently published by the Centre for Research on User Studies[2] which is part of the University there.

It is probably true to say, however, that the pressures which led to the Cawthorpe House conference — largely technological and financial — have given a particular bite and relevance to succeeding activities. The main source of support has been the BLR&D Department and no apologies are made for limiting the contents of this chapter to work funded by it.

The main focus of activity has been the Office for Humanities Communication and its related projects, such as the demonstration sessions on the applications of computers to research in the humanities and the mounting of experimental databases on a microcomputer, all described in Chapter 4.

In addition, the Department supported two small-scale studies — one relating to the current state of computer applications in archives (excluding the Public Records Office)[3]; and a study of the relationship between the content of textbooks and the extent to which they reflect the results of recent research. (This second study has not been reported on at the time of writing.)

The Cawthorpe House conference returned again and again during its discussions to the end user of humanities information. In order that what is known about the 'humanities user' could be discovered, collated and consolidated, the Department commissioned the Centre for Research on User Studies to conduct a review of user-related research and developments in humanities communication. The starting-point of this work, still going on at the time of writing, will be the review article by Stone in *Journal of Documentation*[4], which is being broadened and enhanced. Particular avenues of enquiry are likely to include the user interface with new technology, including microforms, and with abstracts, indexes, guides and other bibliographic aids. There is also, of course, a strong user element in the work of the Office for Humanities Communication. The contacts established by means of its survey work will be kept in being by continued production of the newsletter and by means of special interest seminars and meetings either based on the microcomputer work or exploring more general research needs in individual areas. Taken together, these various initiatives should produce a better appreciation of users' needs and the services which could help them in the future.

The conference also stressed the importance of work on conservation and noted with approval the research programme on conservation supported by the BLR&D Department. The major work in progress at that time has now come to fruition [5], but it is interesting to note that, continuing the theme of the value of binational approaches, the Department supported a visit to the UK by Dr David Stam of New York Public Library, the aim of which was to produce an American overview of policies in the UK on the conservation issue. The report of the visit has been produced [6].

It is also worth noting that, since Cawthorpe, projects which are not primarily related to humanities communication (for example, on referral services in general) are increasingly tending to embrace the humanities in their scope. Hence a greater integration than hitherto is being achieved between research on humanities communication in particular and the wider concerns of the Department with library, information and communication research as a whole.

Readers who may wish to know more about the Department's humanities programme are invited to contact:

Dr R C Snelling,
British Library Research and Development Department,
2 Sheraton Street,
London W1V 4BH.

6.1 References

1   Smith, DB, ed. *Information problems in the humanities: report on the British Library seminar.* London, British Library. 1975. (BL R&D Report 5259.)

2   Stone, S, ed. *Humanities information research: proceedings of a seminar, Sheffield, 1980.* Centre for Research on User Studies, 1980. (BLR&D Report 5588.)

3   Bartle, R and Cook, M. *Computer applications in archives: a survey.* Archives Unit, University of Liverpool, 1983. (BLR&D Report 5749.)

4   Stone, S. Humanities scholars: information needs and uses. *Journal of Documentation,* 38 (4), December 1982, pp 292-313.

5   Ratcliffe, FW with the assistance of Patterson, D. *Preservation policies and conservation in British libraries: report of the Cambridge University Library conservation project.* London, British Library, 1984. (LIR Report 25.)

6   Stam, DH. *National preservation planning in the United Kingdom: an American perspective.* New York Public Library, 1983. (BLR&D Report 5759.)

7 Conclusion

This report has included a number of varied contributions. The authors freely admit that they could even be regarded as disparate. Nevertheless, they also hope that, taken together, the chapters of this report give the reader an awareness of the content and flavour of the rapid developments which have taken place in humanities communication since May 1982, in both the USA and the UK, and also some awareness of the trends and pressures prior to this time, which made some sort of concerted effort essential.

If these trends and pressures, however, created the need for new initiatives, then, certainly, the binational nature of those initiatives has enhanced their momentum and their impact, and, also the enjoyment of those involved in them.

From what has been said in this report it should be clear that, following the conference at Cawthorpe House, the pace of developments in humanities communication has quickened on both sides of the Atlantic. Many of the recommendations resulting from the conference have been pursued in the ways pointed out in Chapters 3 to 6. It would be very wrong, however, for those involved to be too self-congratulatory and complacent. It should also be clear from what has gone before that much still remains to be done — recommendations to be followed up, problems to be solved, data to be gathered, understandings gained. In other words, there is still some way to go before the humanities cease to be the poor relation of the sciences and social sciences in understanding of, investigation into and funding relating to problems in the communication of research. But a start, and a promising start, has been made.

Select bibliography of recent publications on research communication in the humanities

This bibliography is a selection of publications relating to humanities communication which have appeared in the UK and North America in the last few years. Preference has been given to work concerned specifically with the humanities, although it should be noted that relevant material often appears in books and articles about scholarly communication in general. The journals *Scholarly Publishing* and *Computers and the Humanities* are devoted to this subject, and useful current information is to be found in the newsletters of the various organisations concerned, such as the ACLS (*ACLS Newsletter*), the CLR (*CLR Recent Developments*), and the NEH (*Humanities*), and also in *SCOPE*, the newsletter published by the editor of *Computers and the Humanities*.

The bibliography is divided into the following sections:

A. General
B. Libraries, documentation and information services
C. Scholarly publishing
D. Computers and the humanities
E. Individual subjects

    Archaeology
    Art
    History
    Literature and language
    Music
    Religion

The index to the bibliography is included in the general index at the end of this volume; items from the bibliography are distinguished by being in bold type.

The bibliography owes much to a previous list of references compiled for the Cawthorpe House conference by Diana Dixon, Department of Library and Information Studies, University of Loughborough.

A. General

1 Aboyade, BO. Access to primary source material in the humanities. *International Library Review,* 8 (3), July 1976, pp 309-16.

2 *ACLS Newsletter.* A brief history of ACLS activities. 31 (2), Spring 1980, pp 10-19.

3 Banner, JM. American Association for the Advancement of the Humanities. *ACLS Newsletter,* 30 (2/3), Spring/Summer 1979, pp 21-26.

4 Bebout, L and others. User studies in the humanities: a survey and a proposal. *RQ,* 15(1), Fall 1975, pp 40-44.

5 Commission on the Humanities. *The humanities in American life: report of the Commission on the Humanities.* Berkeley, Cal, University of California Press, 1980.

6 Corkill, CM and Mann, MG. *Information needs in the humanities: two postal surveys.* Sheffield, University of Sheffield Centre for Research on User Studies, 1978. (BLR&D Report 5455.)

7 Corkill, CM and others. *Doctoral students in the humanities: a small-scale panel study of information needs and uses 1976-79.* Sheffield, University of Sheffield Centre for Research on User Studies, 1981. (BLR&D Report 5637.)

8 Coward, H. 'Scholarly communication: privileges and responsibilities' in: *Symposium on Scholarly Communication, Ottawa, October 1980.* Ottawa, Social Sciences and Humanities Research Council: Aid to Scholarly Publications Programme, 1981. pp 9-19.

9 Duffey, J. NEH after fifteen years. *ACLS Newsletter,* 31 (2), Spring 1980, pp 3-9.

10 Fabian, B and Vierhaus, R. The calling and condition of the humanistic disciplines. *Minerva,* 17 (4), Winter 1979, pp 549-54.

11 Frankel, C. Why the humanities? *ACLS Newsletter,* 30 (2/3), Spring/Summer 1979, pp 10-20.

12 Hooper, J. Fellowships in the humanities: protecting an endangered species. *Change,* October 1982, pp 43-44.

13 Immroth, J. 'Information needs for the humanities' in: Debons, A, ed. *Information science: search for identity.* New York, Dekker, 1974. pp 249-62.

14 Katzen, M. An office for humanities communication. *Scholarly Publishing,* 14 (2), February 1983, pp 179-86.

15 Kaufmann, W. *The future of the humanities.* New York, Readers Digest, 1977.

16 Lumiansky, RM. The US-USSR Commission on the Humanities and the Social Sciences. *ACLS Newsletter,* 29 (2), Spring 1978, pp 16-22.

17 National Enquiry into Scholarly Communication. *Scholarly communication: the report of the National Enquiry* [by DW Breneman and HC Morton]. Baltimore, JHUP, 1979.

18 Ratcliffe, FW with the assistance of Patterson, D. *Preservation policies and conservation in British libraries: report of the Cambridge University Library conservation project.* London, British Library, 1984. (LIR Report 25.)

19 Smith, DB, ed. *Information problems in the humanities: report on the British Library seminar.* London, British Library, 1975. (BLR&D Report 5259.)

20 Snelling, RC. 'R&D work in retrospect and prospect' in: Stone, S, ed. *Humanities information research: proceedings of a seminar, Sheffield, 1980.* Sheffield, University of Sheffield Centre for Research on User Studies, 1980. pp 7-14.

21 Stam, DH. *National preservation planning in the United Kingdom: an American perspective.* New York Public Library, 1983. (BLR&D Report 5759.)

22 Stone, S. Humanities scholars: information needs and uses. *Journal of Documentation,* 38 (4), December 1982, pp 292-313.

23 Stone, S, ed. *Humanities information research: proceedings of a seminar, Sheffield, 1980.* Sheffield, University of Sheffield Centre for Research on User Studies, 1980. (BLR&D Report 5588.)

24 Sturges, P. Essay review: humanities information research: proceedings of a seminar, Sheffield, 1980. *Social Science Information Studies,* 2 (1), January 1982, pp 39-45.

25 *The Times Higher Education Supplement.* The future of humanities. 416, 24 October 1980, p 31.

B. Libraries, documentation and information services

26 Biggs, M. Sources of tension and conflict between librarians and faculty. *Journal of Higher Education,* 52 (2), 1981, pp 182-201.

Includes humanists' needs and uses of libraries.

27 Bolté, CG. *Libraries and the arts and humanities.* Syracuse, NY, Gaylord, 1977.

28 Broadus, RN and Nielsen, B, eds. *The role of the humanities in the public library.* Chicago, American Library Association, 1979.

29 Buxton, AB and Meadows, AJ. The variation in the information content of titles of research papers with time and discipline. *Journal of Documentation,* 33 (1), March 1977, pp 46-52.

30 Cole, JY. Books, libraries and scholarly traditions. *Scholarly Publishing,* 13 (1), October 1981, pp 31-43.

31 Cox, JM. Self-renewal in the humanities. *New Library World,* 78 (925), July 1977, pp 126-27.

32 Diodato, V. The occurrence of title words in parts of research papers: variations among disciplines. *Journal of Documentation,* 38 (3), September 1982, pp 192-206.

Disciplines include history and philosophy. Has implications for information retrieval.

33 Ellen, SR. Survey of foreign language problems facing the research worker. *Interlending Review,* 7 (2), April 1979, pp 31-41.

34 Fox, PK. *User education in the humanities in US academic libraries.* London, British Library, 1979. (BLR&D Report 5474.)

35 Garfield, E. Is information retrieval in the arts and humanities inherently different from that in science? The effect that ISI's citation index for the arts and humanities is expected to have on future scholarship. *Library Quarterly,* 50 (1), January 1980, pp 40-57.

36 Guy, SMW. *The provision of information services in university and polytechnic libraries in the United Kingdom in the field of humanities: a survey conducted in 1977.* London, British Library, 1977. (BLR&D Report 5379.)

37 Krummel, DW. Introduction to: Trends in the scholarly use of library resources. *Library Trends,* 25 (4), 1977, pp 725-32.

38 Mackesy, EM. A perspective on secondary access services in the humanities. *Journal of the American Society for Information Science,* 33 (3), May 1982, pp 146-51.

39 National Commission on Libraries and Information Science: Public Sector/Private Sector Task Force. *Public sector/private sector interaction in providing information services.* Washington, DC, NCLIS, 1982.

40 Petrey, S. The whole mirth catalogue. *French Review,* 54 (1), October 1980, pp 117-21.

A denunciation of the *Arts and humanities citation index.*

41 Raben, J and Burton, SK. Information systems and services in the arts and humanities. *Annual Review of Information Science and Technology,* 16, 1981, pp 247-66.

42 Soper, ME. Characteristics and use of personal collections. *Library Quarterly,* 46 (4), October 1976, pp 397-415.

43 Thorpe, J. The role of independent research libraries in American society. *ACLS Newsletter,* 31 (3/4), Summer/Fall 1980, pp 1-10.

44 Tucker, PE. The development of research collections in the new university libraries in Britain. *Libri,* 30 (1), 1980, pp 66-81.

45 Walker, GPM. 'Planning, compiling and coordinating guides to resources' in: Stone, S, ed. *Humanities information research: proceedings of a seminar, Sheffield, 1980.* Sheffield, University of Sheffield Centre for Research on User Studies, 1980. pp 61-68.

46 Weintraub, KJ. The humanistic scholar and the library. *Library Quarterly,* 50 (1), January 1980, pp 22-39.

47 Wilson, KB and Eustis, JD. The impact of user frustration on humanities research. *College and Research Libraries,* 42 (4), July 1981, pp 361-65.

48 Wilson, P. Limits to the growth of knowledge: the case of the social and behavioral sciences. *Library Quarterly,* 50 (1), January 1980, pp 4-21.

Includes comparisons with historians.

49 Wilson, P and Farid, M. On the use of the records of research. *Library Quarterly,* 49 (2), April 1979, pp 127-45.

C. Scholarly publishing

50 Bailey, HS. Economics of publishing in the humanities. *Scholarly Publishing,* 8 (3), April 1977, pp 223-31.

51 Budd, J. Humanities journals in 1979. *Scholarly Publishing,* 12 (2), January 1981, pp 171-85.

52 Hardy, H. Viewpoint. *The Times Literary Supplement,* 4057, 26 December 1980, p 1464.

On the reluctance of academic authors to publish, and what the new technology offers.

53 Livesey, F. The market for academic manuscripts. *European Journal of Marketing,* 15 (7), 1981, pp 52-67.

54 Mann, PH. *Author-publisher relationships in scholarly publishing.* London, British Library, 1978. (BLR&D Report 5416.)

55 Meadows, AJ. Current problems in the commercial publishing of scholarly monographs in the United Kingdom. *Journal of Research Communication Studies,* 1 (2), August 1978, pp 125-37.

56 Rodman, H. Some practical advice for journal contributors. *Scholarly Publishing,* 9 (3), April 1978, pp 235-41.

57 Rogers, P. Current and unbound. *The Times Literary Supplement,* 4028, 6 June 1980, p 648.

Discusses the characteristics of scholarly journals in the humanities.

58 Smith, JH. Subvention of scholarly publishing. *Scholarly Publishing,* 9 (1), October 1977, pp 19-30.

D. Computers and the humanities

Computer applications in specific subjects are listed in the following section, E (Individual subjects).

The journal *Computers and the Humanities* (Pergamon Press, Vol 1, 1967 —) is devoted to this subject. It includes an annual bibliography and a *Directory of scholars active* in the field.

59 Battin, P. Research libraries in the network environment: the case for cooperation. *EDUCOM,* 15 (2), Summer 1980, pp 26-31.

60 Borillo, M. Knowledge representation and reasoning in the humanities and social sciences: a conference report. *Computers and the Humanities,* 14 (2), October 1980, pp 115-16.

61 Burnard, LD. At home with the hardware. *The Times Literary Supplement,* 4024, 9 May 1980, p 533.

Reviews the works by Hockey (item 64) and Oakman (item 105).

62 Donati, R. Selective survey of online access to social science data bases. *Special Libraries,* 68 (11), November 1977, pp 396-406.

Includes some humanities databases.

63 Haas, WJ. Computing in documentation and scholarly research. *Science,* 215 (4534), 12 February 1982, pp 857-61.

64 Hockey, S. *A guide to computer applications in the humanities.* London, Duckworth, 1980.

65 Joyce, J. Hardware for the humanist: what you should know and why. *Computers and the Humanities,* 11 (5), September-October 1977, pp 299-307.

66 Lusignan, S and North, JS, eds. *Computing in the humanities: proceedings of the Third International Conference in the*

Humanities ... August 2-6, 1977 at Waterloo, Ontario. Waterloo, University of Waterloo Press, 1977.

67 Patton, PC and Holoien, RA, eds. *Computing in the humanities.* Lexington, Mass, Heath, 1981.

68 Raben, J, ed. 'Computers and the future of humanistic research' in: *Proceedings of the International Conferences on Humanistic Studies, Madrid, 11-16 April 1977.*

69 Raben, J and Marks, GA, eds. *Data bases in the humanities and social sciences.* Amsterdam, North Holland Publishing Co, 1980.

70 Reagor, S and Brown, WS. The application of advanced technology to scholarly communication in the humanities. *Computers and the Humanities,* 12 (3), 1978, pp 237-46.

71 Resnikoff, HL. Implications of advances in information science and technology for institutions of higher learning. *EDUCOM,* 16 (1), Spring 1981, pp 2-6.

72 Seiler, LH, and Raben, J. The electronic journal. *Society,* 18 (6), September/October 1981, pp 76-83.

73 Starr, P. The electronic reader. *Daedalus,* 112 (1), Winter 1983, pp 143-56.

The effects of the new technology on scholarly publishing and the prospects for the future.

74 Stebelmann, SD. 'On-line searching and the humanities: relevance, resistance and marketing strategies' in: *Proceedings of the 2nd National Online Meeting, 24-26 March 1981.* Medford, NJ, Learned Information Inc, 1981. pp 443-53.

E. Individual subjects

Archaeology

75 British Library. *Problems of information handling in archaeology: report of a seminar.* London, British Library, 1977. (BLR&D Report 5329.)

76 McGimsey, CR and Davis, HA, eds. *The management of archaeological resources: the Airlie House report.* Washington, DC, Society for American Archaeology, 1977.

77 Somers, GF. Using NTIS, or how to disseminate archaeological reports. *American Antiquity,* 44 (2), April 1979, pp 330-32.

78 Brady, D and Serban, W. Searching the visual arts: an analysis of online information access. *Online,* 5 (4), October 1981, pp 12-32.

79 Doran, M. 'Research in the RILA British Office' in: Stone, S, ed. *Humanities information research: proceedings of a seminar, Sheffield, 1980.* Sheffield, University of Sheffield Centre for Research on User Studies, 1980. pp 36-44.

80 Ohlgren, TH. The first international conference on automatic processing of art history data and documents: a report. *Computers and the Humanities,* 14 (2), October 1980, pp 113-14.

81 Répertoire International de la Littérature de l'Art (RILA). *Report to the British Library Research and Development Department on the activities of the RILA UK Office 1976-1981.* London, British Library, 1983. (BLR&D Report 5733.)

History

82 Barclay, RL. Access to information with a genealogy and history referral file. *RQ,* 18 (2), Winter 1978, pp 153-55.

83 Bartle, R and Cook, M. *Computer applications in archives: a survey.* Liverpool, University of Liverpool Archives Unit, 1983. (BLR&D Report 5749.)

84 Bogue, AG. The historian and social science data archives in the United States. *Library Trends,* 25 (4), April 1977, pp 847-66.

85 Bradley, I. The problems of getting highbrow history into print. *The Times,* 26 April 1978, p 18.

86 Chapman, J. 'Views of a history information officer' in: Stone, S, ed. *Humanities information research: proceedings of a seminar, Sheffield, 1980.* Sheffield, University of Sheffield Centre for Research on User Studies, 1980. pp 31-32.

87 Collins, B. The computer as a research tool. *Journal of the Society of Archivists,* 7 (1), April 1982, pp 6-12.

88 Elton, GR. Publishing history. *The Times Literary Supplement,* 3876, 25 June 1976, p 764.

89 Falk, JD. Computer-assisted production of bibliographic databases in history. *Indexer,* 12 (3), April 1981, pp 131-39.

90 Falk, JD. 'Searching by historical period in the history databases' in: *Proceedings of the 2nd National Online Meeting, 24-26 March 1981.* Medford. NJ, Learned Information Inc, 1981. pp 199-205.

91 Lytle, RH. Intellectual access to archives. *American Archivist,* 43 (1), Winter 1980, 64-75, pp 191-206.

92 Lytle, RH. A national information system for archives and manuscript collections. *American Archivist,* 43 (3), Summer 1980, pp 423-46.

93 Piehl, CK. Historical research and medium-sized public libraries: the potential. *RQ,* 21 (3), Spring 1982, pp 250-53.

94 Roper, M. New information technology and archives. *Unesco Journal of Information Science, Librarianship and Archives Administration,* 4 (2), April-June 1982, pp 107-13.

95 Smith, C. 'Problems of information studies in history' in: Stone, S, ed. *Humanities information research: proceedings of a seminar, Sheffield, 1980.* Sheffield, University of Sheffield Centre for Research on User Studies, 1980. pp 27-30.

96 Stieg, MF. The information needs of historians. *College and Research Libraries,* 42 (6), November 1981, pp 549-60.

97 Zink, SD. Journal publishing in the field of US history. *Scholarly Publishing,* 11 (4), July 1980, pp 343-59.

Literature and language

98 Ager, DE and others, eds. *Advances in computer-aided literary and linguistic research: proceedings of the Fifth International Symposium on Computers in Literary and Linguistic Research, held at the University of Aston in Birmingham, 3-7 April 1978.* Birmingham, University of Aston Dept of Modern Languages, 1979.

99 Bagnall, RS. *Research tools for the classics.* Chico, Cal, Scholars Press, 1980.

100 Chisholm, D. A survey of computer-assisted research, in modern German. *Computers and the Humanities,* 11 (5), September-October 1977, pp 279-87.

101 Heinzkill, R. Characteristics of references in selected scholarly English literary journals. *Library Quarterly,* 50 (3), July 1980, pp 352-65.

102 Holley, RP. A modest proposal on modern literature collection development. *Journal of Academic Librarianship,* 5 (2), May 1979, pp 91, 94.

103 Jones, A and Churchhouse, R, eds. *The computer in literary and linguistic studies: proceedings of the Third International Symposium.* Cardiff, University of Wales Press, 1976.

104 Mackesy, EM. MLA bibliography on-line provides access to language, literature and folklore. *Database,* 2(3), September 1979, pp 36-43.

105 Oakman, RL. *Computer methods for literary research.* Columbia, SC, University of South Carolina Press, 1980.

106 Sutherland, J. English literary criticism and the commercial publisher: a survey. *British Book News,* February 1978, pp 182-90.

107 Winger, HW. Scholarly use of Renaissance printed books. *Library Trends,* 25 (4), April 1977, pp 733-43.

Discusses the need for original copies, and when microforms or photocopies will do as well.

Music

108 Baker, D. Characteristics of the literature used by English musicologists. *Journal of Librarianship,* 10 (3), July 1978, pp 182-200.

109 Heckmann, H. Computer aids in music libraries and archives. *Fontes Artis Musicae,* 26 (2), April-June 1979, pp 100-101.

110 Wenker, J. 'Creating and maintaining music data bases' in: Raben, J and Marks, GA, eds. *Data bases in the humanities and social sciences.* Amsterdam, North Holland Publishing Co, 1980. pp 269-73.

Religion

111 Choueka, Y. Computerized full text retrieval systems and research in the humanities: the Responsa project. *Computers and the Humanities,* 14 (3), November 1980, pp 153-69.

A project in Rabbinical case-law.

112 Clines, DJA and others. Academic publishing in Biblical studies. *University of Sheffield Newsletter,* 3 (5), 10 January 1979, pp 5-7.

113 Duckett, RJ. Religion on-line or is it? *Bulletin of the Association of British Theological and Philosophical Libraries,* 2, June 1981, pp 6-10.

114 Gorman, GE. Documentation services and information systems of selected religious organizations. *Bulletin of the Association of British Theological and Philosophical Libraries,* 15, 1979, pp 13-15; 16, 1979, pp 9-14.

List of principal acronyms and abbreviations

AAA	American Anthropological Association
AAAH	American Association for the Advancement of the Humanities
AAP	Association of American Publishers
AAU	Association of American Universities
AAUP	Association of American University Presses
ACLS	American Council of Learned Societies
APA	American Philological Association
ARL	Association of Research Libraries
BLR&D	British Library Research and Development
BSDP	Bibliographic Service Development Program
CLR	Council on Library Resources
COSSA	Consortium of Social Science Associations
IEEE	Institute of Electrical and Electronics Engineers
JHUP	Johns Hopkins University Press
LC	Library of Congress
MLA	Modern Language Association of America
MUP	Manchester University Press
NEH	National Endowment for the Humanities
NHA	National Humanities Alliance
NSF	National Science Foundation
OCLC	Ohio College Library Center
RLG	Research Libraries Group
WLN	Washington Library Network

Index

This is an index to the principal people, publications and institutions mentioned in this volume. Numbers in bold type are the numbers of items in the bibliography, not page numbers.

Other reports

Library and Information Research (LIR) Reports may be purchased from Publications Section, British Library Lending Division, Boston Spa, Wetherby, West Yorkshire, LS23 7BQ, UK. Details of previous LIR Reports are given below.

The on-line public library
LIR Report 1   ISBN 0 7123 3002 X
This report describes the establishment, operation and evaluation of the bibliographical information retrieval online service provided for the general public by the Lancashire Library on an experimental basis. Detailed information is provided on project management, searches conducted including times and costs, publicity methods, knowledge and reactions of library staff, user characteristics and evaluation of the services, and document availability and the impact on inter-library loans. Supplementary information is included from a sample survey of staff at the Birmingham Public Library.

Prestel in the public library: reactions of the general public to Prestel and its potential for conveying local information
LIR Report 2   ISBN 0 7123 3003 8
An umbrella cooperative, developed by LASER, involving Prestel sets in 36 public libraries and voluntary organisations during the first year of the full-scale public Prestel service is described. The report seeks to simplify the establishment of similar schemes and to educate potential information providers about Prestel.

Searching international databases: a comparative evaluation of their performance in toxicology
LIR Report 3   ISBN 0 7123 3004 6
The seven major databases in toxicology are compared and evaluated according to the criteria of recall, precision, overlap and currency. In conclusion, guidelines are offered indicating which databases are most useful in particular situations.

The use of patent information in industry
LIR Report 4   ISBN 0 7123 3005 4
This report examines, through case studies, the ways in which patent information is used by individuals in industry and in academic research teams. The fruits of an effort to publicise the patent holdings of Newcastle Central Library are discussed and related to the findings of the case studies.

The state of public library services to teenagers in Britain 1981
LIR Report 5   ISBN 0 7123 3006 2
Looking at the reading habits and tastes of British teenagers, this report scrutinises the response of public libraries to their demands. Policies and attitudes are discussed, and recommendations are made for both current practice and the future.

Prestel in the library context: proceedings of two seminars
LIR Report 6   ISBN 0 7123 3009 7
Two seminars were held, in November 1981, on research involving Aslib, LASER and several public libraries. The uses of Prestel as both source and vehicle of information are discussed.

Optical video disc technology and applications: recent developments in the USA
LIR Report 7   ISBN 0 7123 3010 0
The report recounts a visit to the USA in 1981 to discuss with DiscoVision Associates problems of formatting of material on 35-mm sprocketed roll film to make it compatible with requirements for video disc mastering. Discussions were also held with others on progress in preparing material for such mastering (and experience of use) and in adapting the analogue video disc for digital applications.

Education Advice Service for Adults: a computer database
LIR Report 8   ISBN 0 7123 3011 9
An experiment in supporting Bradford's Education Advice Service for Adults with a small-scale, local, computer-assisted data bank on educational opportunities is described. Using Optel, a model data file was constructed, and the implications of the experience are considered.

Developing information skills in secondary schools: a dissemination project
LIR Report 9   ISBN 0 7123 3012 7
The Centre for Educational Research and Development, Lancaster University set up a two-year project concerned with the development of information skills in secondary schools. The response to the distribution to schools of printed materials on this theme is analysed together with two case studies of individual schools.

Computer software: supplying it and finding it
LIR Report 10   ISBN 0 7123 3014 3
Following the 1981 seminar on 'Libraries and computer materials', a representative survey of the various agencies involved in the production and distribution of computer software was carried out. The results of the survey are used: (a) to give a broad indication of the state of

publishing in this area; and (b) to show the various data elements employed in the description and recording of information about software. An examination of the elements in (b) provides the basis for some observations about cataloguing requirements, and for comparison with existing guidelines.